Cindy Lee Johnson

# DENIS JOHNSON
## SOUL OF A WHORE and PURVIS

Denis Johnson is the author of nine novels, three collections of poetry, and one book of reportage. Between 2000 and 2010, during his stint as Playwright in Residence for the Campo Santo Theater Company at San Francisco's Intersection for the Arts, he wrote six productions for the stage, all premiered by Campo Santo. His novel *Tree of Smoke* was the 2007 winner of the National Book Award.

# ALSO BY DENIS JOHNSON

# SOUL OF
# A WHORE
## AND
# PURVIS

# SOUL OF A WHORE

# AND

# PURVIS

❥ two plays in verse ❧

# DENIS JOHNSON

FARRAR, STRAUS AND GIROUX   NEW YORK

Farrar, Straus and Giroux
18 West 18th Street, New York 10011

Distributed in Canada by D&M Publishers, Inc.
Printed in the United States of America
First edition, 2012

*Soul of a Whore* was previously published, in slightly different form, in *McSweeney's*.
*Purvis* was previously published, in slightly different form, in *The Iowa Review*.

Library of Congress Cataloging-in-Publication Data
Johnson, Denis, 1949–
   [Soul of a whore]
   Soul of a whore ; and, Purvis : two plays in verse / Denis Johnson. —
1st ed.
      p.   cm.
   ISBN 978-0-374-27796-3 (alk. paper)
   1. Verse drama, American.   I. Johnson, Denis, 1949– Purvis.
II. Title.   III. Title: Soul of a whore, and, Purvis.   IV. Title: Purvis.

PS3560.O3745 S58 2012
812'.54—dc23
                                                         2011046069

Designed by Jonathan D. Lippincott

www.fsgbooks.com

1   3   5   7   9   10   8   6   4   2

IN MEMORY OF

LUÍS SAGUAR

# CONTENTS

# SOUL OF
# A WHORE

*Soul of a Whore* was developed by Campo Santo, the resident theater company for San Francisco's Intersection for the Arts (executive director Deborah Cullinan; founders Margo Hall, Luís Saguar, Sean San José, Michael Torres), and premiered at Intersection in February 2003, with the following cast:

| | |
|---|---|
| Donald E. Lacy, Jr. | HT; Dr. Nasum |
| Delia MacDougall | Masha |
| Liam Vincent | Clerk |
| Catherine Castellanos | Granny Black; Nurse Vandermere; Bess Cassandra |
| Brian Keith Russell | Bill Jenks |
| Michael Torres | John Cassandra |
| Marcie Prohofsky | Bus Driver 1; Stacy |
| Alexis Lezin | Bus Driver 2; Jan; Stevie |
| Cully Fredrickson | Sylvester; Will Blaine |
| Danny Wolohan | Simon; Jerry |

Design Team: Suzanne Castillo (costumes), James Faerron (sets), Jim Cave (lighting), Drew Yerys (sound), Dan Hamaguchi (graphics), Jim Roll (original music: "If I Had a Nickel").

Production Team: Jeff Fohl (photography), Melyssa Jo Kelly (assistant lead), Michaela King (assistant), Lena Monje (sound operator), Adam Palafox (research), Honey Roberts (assistant), Elizabeth Rodriguez (costumes assistant), Elizabeth Scott (properties).

Directed by Nancy Benjamin

# CHARACTERS

Masha
HT
Bill Jenks
John Cassandra
Clerk
Granny Black
Sylvester
Simon Blaine
Nurse Vandermere
Will Blaine
Jan Blaine
Stacy Blaine
Dr. Nasum
Jerry Cavenaugh
Stevie
Bess Cassandra
2 Bus Drivers
O.S. Female and Male Voices
O.S. Voice of Jimmy Boggs
O.S. Voice on Radio

*Texas in the years 2000–2002.*

*Scenes might be set through the use of props and a few backdrops.*

*An ellipsis [ . . . ] beginning a line is meant to suggest a pause.*

# PART I

*Dark stage.*

HT's *voice* [*sings*]: *Let the Midnight Special*
    *Shine a light on you*
*Pinpoint spot lights a sign, overhead left: "SURPLUS STORE."*
WOMAN [*O.S.*]: Guys, I need your papers of parole
    And state ID to cash that check, OK?
MAN [*O.S.*]: Dump your whites up there on the second level.
    The second level is where you dump your whites.
    Use the changing room, sir, will you please?
WOMAN [*O.S.*]: Your middle name is printed on that check,
    Then go ahead and spell your whole name out.
    Sign the *back* side: first name, middle name
    If middle name is printed on your check,
    And then your last name; *and* I want your writ
    Of discharge *or* parole certificate
    *And* your official Texas state ID;
    Or else your check will *not* be honored here.
HT's *voice* [*sings*]: *Let the Midnight Special*
    *Shine a ever-lovin' light on you*
*Lights up: Greyhound station in Huntsville, Texas. Plastic*
*pews; standing ashtrays; Coke machine; door to Surplus Store;*
*ticket counter; pay phone.*

CLERK *behind the counter, silent. On the counter a handbell.*
*He bangs it when the mood strikes. Sometimes furtively he nips*
*clear liquid from a screw-top canning jar. He's got a little radio.*

MASHA *talks on the phone. Very brief shiny blue sleeveless*
*dress and big blue platform sandals with white straps. White*
*sunglasses; great big blue-and-white purse.*

HT, *a black man: wants the phone; needs change.*

HT [*sings*]: *Shine a mothaluving light on you* . . .

MASHA [*on phone*]: I *won't* come *back* till *you* stop *mak*ing me—
     OK! Come on!—you just come zooming up
     To Huntsville like some crazed, spawning salmon:
     I'm on my bus before you hit the highway.
     . . . I just don't *want* to. Things like that, they aren't—
     Huh-uh, not de*mean*ing, just, it's more—
     Unnatural. I mean, for me. Or, well,
     For anyone. And I'm not even sure
     I really do it, even when it happens,
     I mean in any verif*i*able . . . "Uh!"
     "Uh uh uh uh uh!"
     Can't you get that worked on, ugly man?
     Can't they drill your head and fix that stutter?
     . . . Your bank account is real. I realize that.
     I truly just don't have the *gift*. I don't.
     There's such a thing as *luck*, you know—like isn't
     Luck what everybody's betting on?
     Wait a minute, got to feed the baby,
     Baby's hungry—[*to* HT] Sir, it's gonna be
     A little while—OK?—'cause I'm addressing
     Certain urgent business—so, could you—?

HT: Man get crazy when his bus don't come.

MASHA [on phone]: If you can hear me, I'm depositing—
HT: I just live in Willard, but the bus
        Won't go there. Got to go see Houston first.
MASHA: "You ever get to Houston,
        Boy, you better walk right."
HT: I will. I do. I got no sheet in Houston.
MASHA: It's just a song.
HT:                    I never been arrested
        Any way or shape or form in Houston.
MASHA: It's just a song. It's just a song.
HT:                                    Lead Belly.
        Sure. I know the song. But I'm just saying.
        —The guys get outa prison yet today?
CLERK: At noon, like always. Bus already left.
HT: Uh-oh. The Houston bus?
CLERK:                    The Dallas bus.
MASHA [on phone]: —No, no! I didn't say the Greyhound station!
        My cousin—good ol' Cousin Gus is coming,
        Not the bus. I wouldn't go by Greyhound
        Ever except in abject desperation!
Meanwhile, an old woman in black enters from street door.
GRANNY BLACK: Hot! Hot! And while I fry in my own fat
        I hear my dead relations singing in Heaven.
        I ain't a-gonna drive on that highway!
        You don't get me behind no chariot wheel!
        Ninety miles of carburetors steaming
        Like cauldrons in a line from here to Dallas.
        Is it carburetors, now? Or radios?
        Or what's the things that steams, where you put water?
CLERK: That'd be the radiator.

GRANNY BLACK:                    Radiator!
    Well!—unless you like that funny music,
    I guess you'd best not wet your radio.
    This is eighteen twenty-five for one
    To Dallas. I won't give a penny more.
    They like to raise the rates with every breath
    They drag, and someone's got to hold the line.
MASHA: . . . No! It ain't the money! Money stinks!
    I haven't got the gift! I haven't got the power!
    Just a minute, let me feed this thing—
    [Deals with coins, etc.]
    Hello? Hello? Hello? *Hello?* HELLO!
    My call is what? Well! You sound sweet as pie!
    You sound just like my mother, operator—
    I want my dollar ten, or you can kiss
    My Rebel ass. —Hung up on by a robot!
    *This* is how the vandalism starts!
CLERK: Now, honey, don't molest my telephone.
    [*To* HT] No. Don't ring the bell. The bell's for me.
HT: Lemme have it all in quarters, please.
CLERK: Try the change machine.
HT:                                It doesn't work.
MASHA [*offering coins*]: Two bucks for a fistful. Gamble.
HT:                                            Thanks.
    You didn't see a guy . . .
CLERK:                        A dozen guys.
    A couple dozen guys. The usual—
    You know. The Dallas took the most of 'em.
    The usual recidivists in transit.

HT: You see a guy, a white guy, maybe looked
    A little not so much a criminal?
CLERK: All human beings look like criminals.
HT *goes to the phone.*
GRANNY BLACK: Hot! Hot! Hear how this poor old woman
        sizzles!
    I pity the crappies and crawdads on account
    I feel now what it hurts like to be cooked.
CLERK: It's twenty dollars fifty cents to Dallas.
GRANNY BLACK: Eighteen twenty-five. No more, no less.
CLERK: It doesn't work that way.
GRANNY BLACK:                    It used to do!
    It used to was a twenty-dollar bill
    *Counted!*—once upon a memory.
    I'll sit down here and let you ponder that . . .
    I'll let you ponder where the whole world went . . .
MASHA: I'm not worried if he's after me.
    By now he's probly halfway out of Texas,
    Blazing a trail for Huntsville, Alabama.
CLERK: Huntsville was named after Huntsville. You knew
        that.
MASHA: Uh—no. I didn't. But it stands to reason.
CLERK: After the one in Alabama. That's
    The explanation for all the confusion, see?
HT [*on phone*]: Hello? It's all— It's jammed. Hello?
        Completely.
    Fine. You busted it. Are you content?
MASHA: I'm just as happy as a clam in shit.
HT: O yeah? I think you got that saying wrong.

MASHA: I think you never saw a clam in shit.

HT: When's the Houston come?

CLERK:                              It comes as scheduled.

HT: Scheduled when?

CLERK:                   It's not that type of schedule.
        It's theoretical. Four a day.

HT:                                  In theory.

CLERK: No, the vehicles themselves are real,
        But all the rest is veiled in mystery
        Because from here to goodness idiots
        Are tearing up the road and moving it
        West eleven inches. Traffic's stuck
        For hours at a time in all directions:
        Miles and miles of stationary drivers
        Contemplating this minute adjustment.

HT: Sound like the joint.

CLERK:                   It kinda does, at that.

HT: You been inside?

HT *gets himself a Coke.*

MASHA:                    . ... He'll hop the barricades.
        He'll ride the back roads and the shoulder, then
        He'll drive on top of all the other cars.
        He will. He's on his way. I get no rest.

HT: Gah-dam, gah-dam, gah-*dam!*

CLERK:                              Excuse me, sir.

HT: I think it might be eating me *alive.*

CLERK: Crazy folks are not allowed in here.

HT: Crazy folks are *too* allowed in here.
        Is this the Greyhound stop in Huntsville, Texas?—
        Crazy folks get born and *die* in here.

CLERK: I know you, sir. They call you Hostage Taker.

HT: Yeah, yeah, it's good to see you, good to see you.
Man, the bus don't come and the bus don't *come*.
Man, I got to get on down the *road*.
Man, this whole block used to jump with gypsy
Hot-shot cabs'll take you there right *now*—
For twenty bucks they're gonna fly to Houston,
Dallas, anyplace on earth—and they
Got *reefer*, they got *beer*, they got te*qui*la—

CLERK: I thought they sprung you couple months ago.

HT: Sooner or later all God's chillun be free.
[*Raises his Coke*]
"Wardens, jailers, presidents and kings—
They all must bow to calendars and clocks."

CLERK: Then what puts you in Huntsville not a block
From where you did hard time? Guilt? Or nostalgia.
Or some concoction of the two.

HT: Touché!

CLERK: Touché?

HT: Touché! That's what you say! You say
"Touché!" when someone jabs you with a word.

CLERK: I jabbed you what? I jabbed—

HT: You see . . .
You dig . . . You don't begin your day with things
Like taking hostages on the agenda.
"Things to Do: Do NOT take hostages."
You march inside, extend your weapon towards
The various faces, and receive the money.
PO-lice DO not COME sahROUND-ing you!
Megaphones and telephones and shit!

And no one's hurt! And NO ONE GOES TO PRISON.

. . . I'm waiting on a guy. But I can't wait.

CLERK: If you can't wait, I guess you're better off

To don't. So see you later, Hostage Taker.

MASHA: I thought you said the bus—you live in—where?

HT: I never tell the truth. It's too confusing.

You wanna get a drink? Or take a walk?

Something? Maybe feel the feelings of

The outside world? Fresh air?

MASHA: No thanks, I'm good.

HT: I didn't mean—

MASHA: I know.

HT: I didn't mean—

MASHA: But I'm just comfortable. I'm good right here.

HT *exits through Surplus Store.*

CLERK: Now, there's a guy got bubbles in his brain.

. . . Well, looky here: The show's not over, folks.

BILL JENKS *enters from the street door.*

MASHA: You are *sucking* on me with your *eyes.*

You're staring like a laser beam.

BILL JENKS: My wife was here

She'd read my mind and kill me on the spot.

. . . Did I hear someone singing, while ago?

CLERK: Just some bubble-brain with vocal cords.

BJ *offers* MASHA *a smoke. She ignores it; finds her own.*

BILL JENKS: You hang around the Greyhound all the time?

MASHA: Don't mistake me, hon.

BILL JENKS: For what?

MASHA: For what you think.

BILL JENKS: And what am I thinking?

MASHA:                                        That's for me to know.

*She lights his smoke.*

BILL JENKS [*smoking*]: I'm ready to believe in God again!

MASHA: Could you, like, hold the revival over there?

BILL JENKS: The gods combust our dreams for sport and suck
     The fumes. Our spirits serve as censers.

MASHA:                                                Shit.
     You dudes are never right when you come out.
     [*Smoking*] What's a censer?

BILL JENKS:                              It's the—hell, *you* know—
     Those things they burn the incense in at Mass?
     Come on, don't kid around—a name like Masha—

MASHA: From where do you know my name?

BILL JENKS:                                    From here.
     I overheard. Your lovely back was turned.
     You breathed your name into the telephone.

MASHA: That was my boss! I didn't breathe a-tall!

BILL JENKS: Masha's Russian. You could be Orthodox:
     They're always swinging censers.

MASHA:                                   Let 'em swing,
     'Cause I ain't Russian! I'm from Texas, son.

BILL JENKS: So where'd you get the Masha from? Odessa?

MASHA: Hell if I know. It's my name, is all . . .
     You're not from Texas.

BILL JENKS:                    No, ma'am. Mississippi.
     But I was mostly raised in California.
     Don't get me wrong, I love you Texas women.

MASHA: How long were you in prison for? This time?

BILL JENKS: What makes you think I've been incarcerated?

MASHA: The checkered pants, the polo shirt, those big
    Enormous shoes, no belt, that stubbly head—
    The outa prison used-up fashion show.

BILL JENKS: They don't have threads like these in prison, doll.
    Except the shoes. And shoes like these are common.

MASHA: You cashed your fifty at the Surplus Store
    And dumped your whites and bought the nearest thing.
    Last week the streets were full of guys with boot-camp
    Haircuts sporting stripèd Ban-Lon shirts
    And almost iridescent green bell-bottoms.
    Pouring rain outside, and here they come,
    This mob of palpitating free men kind of
    Trailing a verdant dribble off their cuffs.
    Their T-shirts shrank right on them as we watched.

BILL JENKS: "Palpitating"? "Verdant"? What a smarty.
    "What's a censer?" What a smarty pants.
    Ain't you a genius. Where'd you go to school?

MASHA: I didn't go. I didn't need to go.

BILL JENKS: You knew it all.

MASHA:                 Enough to not get busted.

BILL JENKS: But not to not divide infinitives.

MASHA: Fucked-up grammar is not a crime in Texas.

*He smokes. Offers one. She ignores it.*

BILL JENKS: They cost a buck apiece inside . . . How much are
    you?

MASHA: I dance. I'm not for sale. I dance.

BILL JENKS:                   You strip.

MASHA: I'm not exactly a ballerina, no.

BILL JENKS: But you done quit the life. Or so I heard.

MASHA: Heard when? When I was on the telephone?

BILL JENKS: Yeah, and I could smell the putrid karma
Percolating in the interaction,
And I say this: Whatever's going on
With you and him can only improve with distance.

MASHA: I didn't see you around. Just prisoners.

BILL JENKS: One was me. And then I bought the outfit . . .
Pack of smokes . . . and we're not prisoners.
We're out—How do!—We move among you now.

MASHA: What were you in for? Dealer? Killer?—Rapist.

BILL JENKS: Victim of religious persecution.

MASHA: Jewish, huh?

BILL JENKS:              I was irregular.

MASHA: And went to prison for it?—What'd you do,
Diarrhea all over somebody?

BILL JENKS: My *conduct* was irregular. That is,
With money.

MASHA:              Sure. You stuck somebody up.

BILL JENKS: I was convicted of commingling funds.
It means a stick-up with a ballpoint pen.

MASHA: Do tell. Co-mingling funds. Is that Chinese?

BILL JENKS: Lady, is that the way you play your game?
Hang around the Greyhound lookin' down,
Makin' fun of other folks's clothes—
And Masha is a Russian nickname, sis.

MASHA: No, it's not. "Sis" is a nickname. Masha's
What I got at birth. My name is Masha.

BILL JENKS: . . . *Mar*-sha—!

MASHA:              Yeah . . .

BILL JENKS:                        Well, I like Masha better.

MASHA: When I dance I'm Fey or I'm Yvette
    Or I'm Nicole and then I'm naked.

BILL JENKS:                       Naked!

MASHA: I start out topless and proceed from there,
    And logic does the rest.

BILL JENKS:              I'll bet it does.
    I'll bet it ends up running down the road
    Yodeling and firing off both guns.

MASHA: You're pretty slick with words.

BILL JENKS:                 Ain't but a tic.

MASHA: I'll bet your mouth gets you in trouble. Lots.

BILL JENKS: And where would someone fresh from prison go
    To watch you executing logic so
    Ruthlessly and gracefully? To Heaven?
    Or someplace even higher?

MASHA:               Try the Texas.

BILL JENKS: The Texas Bar?

MASHA:            The Big-As-Texas.

BILL JENKS:                   ... O!—
    Sylvester's Big-As-Texas Topless Lounge!
    I guess I wasn't off by very much:
    "Just fifty miles from Houston and right next
    To Paradise on Highway 35."
    How do you get to and from? You got a car?

MASHA: No, but I can always catch a ride.

BILL JENKS: I do believe you can. I guarantee it.
    And what's your next stop? Dallas?

MASHA:                 I'm not sure.

BILL JENKS: Not sure?

MASHA:          I need to pick the proper move.
      It's heads or tails, and devil take the hindmost.
BILL JENKS: Sounds like you better grab the first thang smokin'.
MASHA: The *tips* were big as Texas—then the road
      Got all torn up, and now it's like a tomb,
      And I got Peter Lorre for a boss, who just
      Keeps jacking up the price of doing business.
BILL JENKS: I guess that happens all the time.
MASHA:                                    Huh-uh,
      It ain't what you imagine. It's much weirder,
      Wilder—*unnatural*—and no, no, no,
      It still ain't what you're thinking. It's not sex.
      . . . You mentioned a wife.
BILL JENKS:                    O! Yeah. I probly did.
      And did I mention that her lawyers mentioned
      A divorce?
MASHA:          It wasn't really necessary.
BILL JENKS: You turn me on. I think you make me wild.
      Smart women get me going. Thus my downfall.
MASHA: Step right up and blame it on a woman . . .
      How long did Texas guard your purity?
BILL JENKS: One and one-sixth years. That's fourteen months.
      —And I went in there in a monastic spirit:
      I've been voluntarily celibate,
      And celibate, God willing, I'll remain.
MASHA: Well, you've been talking like your holy vow
      Escaped your mind and pulled your trousers down.
BILL JENKS: Matter of fact it did. Wow. Fourteen months.
      . . . I like the way your heel's a little dirty.

I like the way you point your toes. I like
That silvery sort of robot-colored sort of
Sequined toenail polish.

MASHA:                                    You are sick!

BILL JENKS: Wow. Just the sight of your foot makes me drool.
Your human foot. Wow. Fourteen months locked up.

MASHA: Aren't there any humans with feet in there?

BILL JENKS: Humans? Yeah. Humans too goddamn human:
Misused and violent Negroes, and abused
And violent Texas crackers, and confused
Bilingual Meskin desperados—also
Violent—and sweet, retarded boys
Who can't recall the violence they've done . . .
Deranged mulattos, and mestizos scrambled
In their natural brains . . .
Saints and suckers stirring in a stew
Of HIV and hepatitis C and walls
And years. And, yes: I guess they've all got feet.
But none of them ever dreamed of a foot like yours.

MASHA: You're not a lover, are you . . . You're a preacher . . .

BILL JENKS: Fourteen months exactly to the minute,
The same as Elvis did in *Jailhouse Rock*.
[*He goes to the counter.*]
Got me a voucher for the Dallas bus.

CLERK: Dallas'll be along behind the Houston.

BILL JENKS: The Houston bus came not an hour ago.

CLERK: The Dallas end of things is crumbling.
While Texas undertakes repairs, there's just
This formless ooze of throbbing vehicles

From here to there and back that never moves . . .
(I would love to strafe those motherfuckers . . . )
BILL JENKS: That lady got a pulse?
CLERK:                              That's Granny Black,
      Mourning her man who died in the electric chair.
      Yeah, she was young and wild. And he was wilder.
      Crazy little gambler with a temper.
      Shot four niggers in a poker game,
      Killed 'em all though he held the winning hand.
      Well, you could get away with shooting one
      Or two along back then around these parts,
      But even colored you can't slaughter by
      The dozens and not expect to meet Joe Byrd.
MASHA: Joe Byrd?
CLERK:            The man with the electric chair.
BILL JENKS: The executioner for fifty years
      Or something like that.
CLERK:                        Captain Joseph Byrd—
      The guy they named the cemetery after,
      The resting place for prisoners, I mean.
      He executed seven hundred men.
BILL JENKS: Well—not quite seven hundred.
CLERK:                                  It was plenty—
      You want facts and figures, read a book.
      She walks among the graves up there all night.
      Yeah. She's a cheerful, harmless thing in daylight.
      Always dickering on the price to Dallas.
      Never has the price. Just comes to talk
      And settle down and sleep all afternoon.

Nights you'll spy her drooling on his grave,
Wailing for the Resurrection, weeping.
But ain't she sweet and harmless in the daylight?

BILL JENKS: Do you know what? If something moved you to,
If curiosity prompted you, or pity,
You could take three hundred steps from that
Gray bench in those pretty blue shoes and stand
Exactly in the holy chamber where
Tonight they'll execute a human being.

MASHA: I read about it. Hey. If guys like you
Weren't punished, where'd we be? All you
Deranged and violent mulattos and
Your numerous other friends. If you
Were just forgiven, where would we be then?

BILL JENKS: In Heaven. Watching Masha shake her thang . . .
Look. In the joint the cereal don't go
Snap crackle pop. It pewls and moans.
The dogs don't go bow-wow. They say, Achtung!
They say, Jawohl! Sieg Heil! et cetera.
The whistle doesn't blow. It reams your brains.

MASHA: They have a whistle?

CLERK:                                 Lady, they sure do.

BILL JENKS: Every morning, middle of your dreams.
You maybe did a little stretch?

CLERK:                                 Why, no . . .

MASHA: I never got your name.

BILL JENKS:                                 Name's Bill. Bill Jenks.

MASHA: You realize your initials are "BJ."

BILL JENKS: It hadn't escaped my attention entirely, no.

MASHA: . . . So you're a preacher. Or you used to be.

BILL JENKS: So I don't look familiar? Not at all?
     Really?
MASHA:     I very seldom cruise the links.
BILL JENKS: Don't you watch the TV?
MASHA:                    I'm the show.
BILL JENKS: It happens I was poorly represented.
MASHA: Legally or journalistically?
BILL JENKS: Both ways. And up and down and back and forth.
     When schism racks a flock, some sheep are torn.
     The shepherd too sometimes. That's showbiz, folks.
MASHA: Shepherd or showman?
BILL JENKS:                    Shaman,
     Shaman of the Children of Jehovah.
     My scheme went wrong. My streetcar hopped the track.
     A woman was the ripple in the rail.
MASHA: Were you a preacher or an engine driver?
BILL JENKS: I was a shaman, babe, a shaman with a scheme.
MASHA: Shepherd, shaman, engine driver—hey,
     All I know—you just got outa prison.
BILL JENKS: . . . *Crimes* . . . No . . . *Love* . . . *Love* . . . Let me
     make my case . . .
MASHA: O, Jesus Christ! *Love!* That's a crazy word—
     Ain't no bigger than a postage stamp,
     But go to pry the corner up, you're peeking
     Upon a continent.
BILL JENKS:               OK, OK,
     I rest my case.
MASHA:               What case?
BILL JENKS:                    Hell, *I* don't know.
     If I had courtroom skills, I'd be a judge.

I wouldn't be no puppy-blind parolee
Strolling around in pegged and checkered pants.
At least they fit.

MASHA: At least you think they do.

BILL JENKS: Come on now, Masha, honey, have a heart.

MASHA: Look, I've got a heart, and I've got feeling
For the luckless, and I've even got two cousins
Locked up—or one; they let the other loose.
But I've got troubles too, that's all. OK?

BILL JENKS: You think I didn't know that? It's the Greyhound.
This train don't carry no senators' sons.
. . . God. Is it possible . . . on this day of days?
. . . OK. It is. I'm sitting here . . . I'm drowning.
To think the dropdown blues could ambush you
The day they pour you from a prison cell,
First day in years you own your own footsteps,
First day the breezes carry a whiff of choice—
Fifty bucks, your hair growing back,
Your feet up, waiting for the two p.m.
To Dallas, and drowning. A guy should be ashamed,
You know? Humanity should be ashamed.

MASHA: Because you didn't want to leave them there.

BJ *purchases a Coke and sadly raises a toast:*

BILL JENKS: Negroes, Meskins, Crackers, and Mulattos—
"Wardens, jailers, presidents and kings—
All must bow to calendars and clocks."
I raise to you one ice-cold Coca-Cola . . .
Shoot, I drank this stuff inside. Somebody
Bring me something civilized!—a pale
Green olive sharing a freezing bath

Of Gordon's with a solitary molecule
Of sweet vermouth. I mean I like 'em dry.
Can I get a "Hell yes"?

CLERK: *Hell* yes!

MASHA: *Hell* . . .

BILL JENKS: Good . . . Low-erd . . .

*Meanwhile,* JOHN CASSANDRA *enters: large, rounded, slouching; somewhat the biker, but shaved and shorn and wearing prison-issue whites and work shoes.*

*He totes a wooden cross taller than himself, his shoulder in the crotch of the crossbeam. This burden rolls along on casters fixed to its base.*

MASHA: What—a—blowjob!

JOHN *makes his way slowly toward the ticket counter.*

BILL JENKS: I think my order has been misconveyed.
I asked for liquor. Not the crucifixion.
I seek libation. Not religion. Well,
Howdoo, Christian? —Or do I assume too much?

MASHA *takes a seat and stares in shiny-eyed silence at John.*

JOHN [*to* CLERK]: This here's a Dallas voucher, from the
Walls.

BILL JENKS: You bought that thing!

JOHN: Bought it or stole it, one.
. . . Keep your sights!
In the heights!
Keep your eyes!
On the prize!

BILL JENKS: . . . I saw that gizmo leaning in a houseyard.
I didn't inquire was it available—
Not to imply I'd have availed myself.

JOHN: The sign said "For Sale." The man named his price. I
    paid it.

BILL JENKS: You blew your fifty bucks on Jesus.

JOHN:                                        Yep.

BILL JENKS: On Jesus Christ, the famous savior guy.

JOHN: I didn't blow it on checkered pants and cancer.

BILL JENKS: Now, here's a man resists the cigarettes,
    A man with strength to stand against such things
    As checkered pants and, he'd have us assume,
    The random crimson Ban-Lon shirt. But, now:
    While golfing, aren't you known to make a wager?

JOHN: I don't gamble, no. But I'd play golf
    If someone ever thought to ask me to.
    They'd have to show me how it works—you know—
    They'd have to point me down the fairlane.

BILL JENKS: O Holy One: You ever take a drink?

JOHN: Not the alcoholic kind.

BILL JENKS:                 OK.

JOHN: Or not no more, at least.

BILL JENKS:                Uh-oh.
    That Not No More can get to be Right Now
    Right quick the day they let you out of jail.

JOHN: I know. I gotta keep my eyes on Heaven.
    Keep your sights!
    On the heights!
    Keep your eyes!
    On the prize!—

BILL JENKS: —Hey. Martin Luther. What about tattoos?
    What kind you got? Describe us your tattoos.

JOHN: There's not a one. I wouldn't mark my body.

BILL JENKS: Come on. You've gotta have one swastika.
One Born to Raise Hell. And at least one silly
Very Dixie-sounding woman's name
In a vague and fading heart—like Sally,
Sally June. Or Junie May. Come on,
What's the name inside your heart?

JOHN:                                        It's Jesus.
Jesus Christ.

BILL JENKS:        O-K. —You want a Coke
Before your bus? Before we nail you up?

JOHN: No, thanks.

MASHA:        No, thanks, "BJ." —Now, there's
A nickname you don't want to take to prison.

CLERK *hands* JOHN *a ticket.*

CLERK: One to Dallas. Be about an hour.

BILL JENKS: Give or take.

JOHN:                        I see your radio.
Your radio?

CLERK:        Well, I'm not hiding it.

JOHN: I was gonna ask to have it on.

CLERK: No sir. Nope. Got *way* way too much static
Cluttering up the air in here already.
I'm gonna have to make it policy.

JOHN: Just at the hour? Just to catch the news?
You could listen—look, I hate to ask—
And you could tell me what the news is saying.
They're ruling on my mom today . . . My mother.
Today's her last appeal. She's on Death Row.
I hate to ask.

CLERK:        Also I hate to say:

We execute great swarms of people here.

No—we don't fool around down here in Huntsville.

Try 'em and fry 'em.

BILL JENKS: Boys, don't mess with Texas.

CLERK: This is an appeal?

JOHN: Appeal, that's right.

CLERK: She's already on Death Row.

JOHN: Correct. She is.

CLERK: So she'd be—well, you've got two females

Waiting on the reaper up in Gatesville,

And Alice Allenberry's way too young

To be your mom—so she'd be Bess Cassandra.

JOHN: Correct. That's her.

BILL JENKS: Cassandra! *There's* a name.

CLERK: The one who killed Jane Doe. Known as

"The Jane Doe Killer."

JOHN: Now you're *not* correct.

You're absolutely *wrong*. That's *false*.

She's innocent.

CLERK: Like you. Like mom, like son.

JOHN: In one quick life I couldn't do the time

For even half my sins, for just a small-

Size portion of the ones that I forget.

But I've been baptized and, you know—new-minted,

Thanks to prison preaching. Not my mom.

My mom's not baptized. She's just innocent.

Her hands are clean. She didn't kill that girl.

CLERK: I'm really not the one to tell. Greyhound

Doesn't hire clerks to sit in judgment.

JOHN: You think they care who killed that girl?

She was in for worse stuff than my mom.
They needed to close the book on it, they needed
A simple picture for the media,
And so they put my mother in a frame.
CLERK: Hey, I don't sit here judging. All I know
Is what the TV wants for me to know,
Like all Americans everywhere. That girl
Was sort of innocent, too—I mean, the years
Of booze and dope had bleached her brain to white,
To where she couldn't even tell her name.
She'd woken up in bed with some deceased
Farmer with the handle of a dagger
Jutting from his neck—or, I don't know,
A belly full of buckshot—anyhow,
The whole bed squishy with his murdered gore
And this amnesiac harlot rolling in it
Like a log in a flood. So, you say the crimes
You can't remember? Well, she did her time
Without a memory of *any*thing, until
Another prisoner kills her with a broomstick.
These are the details of a blameless life.
And if your mother's blameless, too, another
Innocent heading for the axe—all right:
Now you know what universe you're in.
But I will listen to the radio.
BILL JENKS: For I've been purged with tears! Baptized by water!
Washed in saving blood! And turned out blank
And white as platinum on a sunny morning—
[*As* FIRST BUS DRIVER *enters*]
Which bus is this?

CLERK: The Magic Bus, I guess,
Materializing most miraculously.
Have I got everybody's vouchers here?
Has everybody got their tickets? [*To* MASHA] Ma'am?
He's gonna want a ticket. Ma'am?

DRIVER 1: OK,
I'm hardly pausing to relieve myself.
Line 'em up and march 'em on, let's roll.
Folks, come on, I haven't got till Xmas.
You wanna get your big old cross aboard?

JOHN: I didn't think you'd haul it.

DRIVER 1: Crosses, stars,
Hearts-and-arrows, circles, figure eights—
It pays, it rides. This ain't no limousine.

BILL JENKS: This ain't no paradise.

MASHA: This ain't no blowjob!

DRIVER 1: Hey, Patoot. You better curb the lingo.
'Board for Houston, Texas! Rock and roll!

JOHN: But I don't go to Houston, Mr. Driver.

DRIVER 1: Today you do. The northbound lanes have had it.
You want the Dallas bus, then be prepared
To languish. This day, everybody's Houston.
Yeah—sooner or later, everybody's Houston.
Git it while you can! Last call for Houston!

DRIVER 1 *exits*.

BILL JENKS: Sooner or later Houston gets us all.

CLERK: Well, sorry—I can't rewrite all y'all:
Your vouchers say to Dallas. And, now, ma'am:
I'd like to write you up for Dallas, since
The fact is otherwise you're loitering.

MASHA: Fact is I know a blowjob when I see one.

Fact is I'm here to use the phone.

*Sound of bus leaving.*

CLERK: There she goes . . . She didn't waste no time.

Folks, we're on the bus schedule from Hell.

BJ *extends his hand to* JOHN.

BILL JENKS: William Jennings Bryan Jenks. The first.

JOHN: That's funny. 'Cause my dad is named like that:

Oliver Wendell Homes Cassandra . . . Yeah.

BILL JENKS: Cassandra. There's a name I've always hated.

JOHN: Also the first. His folks misspelled it, though.

BILL JENKS: Misspelled "the first"?

JOHN:                                         No. "Holmes."

BILL JENKS:                              Don't call me Holmes.

This ain't the 'hood.

JOHN:                              No—They forgot the *L*.

H-O-L-M-E-S. Get it? "Holmes."

BILL JENKS: Don't call me Holmes. I ain't your homey, John.

JOHN: Don't call me John. Aah—

BILL JENKS:                              Well, then, what's your name?

JOHN: —Shit. It's John. But not like *that*, I mean.

Just call me John like *John*. Like it's my *name*.

BILL JENKS: I see. And—missing any letters, John?

JOHN: My dad is missing the *L* in his, is all.

BILL JENKS: "Oliver Wendell Homes Cassandra." Wow.

I think your family may be known to me.

You wouldn't have a brother?

JOHN:                              I'd have two.

BILL JENKS: Would one be Mark?

JOHN:                              We call him Cass.

BILL JENKS: I had some dealings with a Mark Cassandra
        From California. Actually, I shot him.
        Actually, more than once. I shot him twice.
        Not twice on one occasion—once
        On each of two quite separate occasions.
        Once by mistake—the second time, on purpose.
        Popped him like a Coney Island clown.
JOHN: I know all about it. He's my brother.
BILL JENKS: Mark Cassandra.
JOHN:                          Yes, sir. Mark Cassandra.
BILL JENKS: I don't think we're going to be friends.
A SECOND BUS DRIVER *enters.*
DRIVER 2: Folks, I got as many seats as you got butts
        To fill 'em up, but what I lack is time
        To mess around and all, so git along,
        And all aboard, and off we go, and so on.
JOHN: Ma'am, can you point me where to put this cross?
DRIVER 2: I don't believe I will. That's not allowed.
        The glory train don't carry no religious
        Signifying statues of any type,
        No banners, emblems, images, or icons,
        No crosses, crescents, Hebrew hexagrams,
        No Guadalupey Ladies, no Buddhistic
        Eight-armed elephants from Hindustan;
        None but the uncreated, changeless, true,
        Eternal, kind of gray and kind of blue
        Dog in flight. I guess you could say pewter.
        Pewter is the color of the greyhound.
        Houston! Austin! San Antonio!

JOHN: You're going to *Houston*, is it, ma'am?

BILL JENKS:                                     Far—out.

JOHN: But—what about the bus to Dallas?

DRIVER 2:                                     Houston,
        Houston, Texas! San Antonio!

JOHN: But we just had a gal in here announced
        That *she* was the Houston bus.

DRIVER 2:                                     Nope. She was Dallas.
        A Dallas driver will generally lie.
        That's why I stay the heck away from Dallas.
        Heck, they killed the president in Dallas.
        Houston's the place you need to be.

BILL JENKS: But then, of course, *you* could be lying, too.

DRIVER 2: That's absolutely the case. You're catching on.
        Yes. I could be a lying Dallas driver . . .
        Aboard for Houston! If thou dost believe!
        [*Exits; fading O.S.*]
        . . . Ten nine eight seven six five four three two . . .

*Sound of bus leaving.*

JOHN: This is total bullshit. Nothing less.

BILL JENKS: If they can mess with you, they mess with
        you.
        That's a fact of nature here in Texas—
        I'm speaking as a Mississippian—
        But, also: Don't you ask for disrespect
        By traveling your way in prison whites?
        I speak now as a Mississippian
        With nothing but the highest, deepest, fullest
        Regard for your West Coast Cassandra clan,

Excluding, naturally, that full-on, rank,

Hellborn, Hellbound slut-soul, your brother Mark,

Who spawned his own self fucking his own mother.

JOHN: That's some rowdy talk! You better hope

The prison preaching holds, and I stay Christian!

BILL JENKS: I'd never've done my time without that kid

Making himself such goshdarn fun to shoot.

JOHN: He dropped the charges.

BILL JENKS:                          That was good of him—

JOHN: He'd never send a guy to jail. He's just

A crook himself. But, now, revenge—

Revenge is something I'd be counting on.

It's truly amazing he passed up on that;

It's basically miraculous he failed

To hunt you down and gut you like a frog.

BILL JENKS: He did run me to ground—the second time.

That's partly why I let him have another.

The first time was by accident, and then

Instead of letting bygones just be bygones,

Here he comes *again*—

JOHN:                          To make *amends*.

. . . That's right. My brother's sober now

About a year and seven months: I'm *proud*.

BILL JENKS: Amends? Amends?

JOHN:                          Like in the twelve-step program.

Number nine, you go and make amends.

BILL JENKS: Alcoholics Anonymous, you mean?

He never said.

JOHN:                 You didn't let him say.

BILL JENKS: Then let *me* say the little lunatic

Stole near a pound of my cocaine, then *flushed* it.

How was he going to make amends for that?

*They're squaring off*—CLERK *intervenes*—

CLERK: John Cassandra!—well, they cut your hair

And shaved your beard, but I think you're the man

Stood on the roof of a parking ramp in Dallas

Shooting folks and threatening suicide.

JOHN: I didn't shoot nobody.

CLERK:                                   Shooting *at*.

JOHN: In the *direction* where they *were*, let's say—

BILL JENKS: I guess it's fortunate no Kennedys

Happened to be strolling by that day.

CLERK: Just settle down. Just settle down. RIGHT NOW.

JOHN: I'm willing to. I didn't come for this.

CLERK: I can get you back in prison quick!

JOHN: *He's* the one who's escalating from

A simple conversation to a riot!

—Why? Because you want to stop your ears.

BILL JENKS: I what? I what?

JOHN:                                 You want to stop your ears

And hide your heart from the Holy Spirit's prompting.

BILL JENKS: Come again? Sorry—my ears are stopped—

JOHN: Peruse the facts: You shoot my brother twice,

He lets you skate, but you get busted later,

Exactly at the proper time and place

To land you in the Walls the same as me,

And get you *out* the same as me, and put you *here*—

The same as me. Is this coincidence?

You and I are strangled up together.
We've got our fates in a knot. And here we stand.
Guided by the Holy Spirit, here we stand.

BILL JENKS: I ain't the quickest rabbit in the pack,
I guess the record proves that much, but, God,
I hope to Christ by now I've learned enough
To leave that Holy Spirit shit alone.

JOHN: Look. I recognized you. You knew that.
I recognized your face a year ago,
My first day on the yard. I watched you stand
Exactly still, more left-out and alone
Than any creature there, not halfway in
Your own skin, more the newcomer
Than me—but you'd been there two months.
Never saw a prisoner looked so much
Like somebody in prison. Every inch
And ounce of you in bondage. Sure, they had
The background on you, all the Christian bunch,
But nobody could figure out your story—
The famous shaman, healer of multitudes,
Standing in the yard with this, like, music
Coming down around your head, this
Jazz falling apart around you, man . . .
Look, my mother, I . . . my mother, sir . . .

BILL JENKS: There's nothing I can do to help your mother.

JOHN: You have the gift, you have the power to heal,
You can help whoever you decide.
Don't you see, you're touched by the same fingers
That turn the earth.

BILL JENKS:　　　　　Well, tell the fingers to get
　　　Their claws outa me! . . . I can't help your mother!
MASHA *bangs the receiver against the pay phone unit repeatedly.*
MASHA: WHAT! A BUNCH! A MOTHAH! FUCKIN! COCK-
　　　SUCK!
　　　GAAAAAAAAH!
　　　[MASHA *strikes the machine harder and harder. She
　　　doesn't stop.*]
　　　WAAAAAAAAH!!!
　　　[*Keeps beating the machine. Sings like Bessie Smith:*]
　　　GIMME A REEFAH
　　　AND A GANG A GIN
　　　SLAY ME 'CAUSE I'M IN MY SIN!
　　　[*She's berserk, assaulting the phone.*]
　　　YAAAAAAAAAAAAAH!!
*Simultaneously, the* CLERK *erupts.*
CLERK: I have HAD IT HAD IT HAD IT HAD IT, BOY.
　　　Do you think I'm more than human?
　　　I've only got two hands!
　　　I can't take care of everything at once!
　　　I don't have superstrength and X-ray eyes
　　　To deal with you-all! I'm not Superman!
　　　I'm not Captain Marvel! I'm not the Hulk!
　　　To drag myself each morning from sweet dreams
　　　Into your sleazy Greyhound station nightmare
　　　Of God-forsaken apparitions with
　　　Madness and sadness congealing in their eyes
　　　And sell them TICKETS TICKETS TICKETS TICKETS!
　　　Look at this!—Look at this woman doing

All a human can to destroy that thing!

Nothing stands between the realm of sanity

And total chaos but myself alone!

I'm all alone at the bulwarks of the world!

MASHA: HAAAAAAAH!! GAAAAAAAHHHHHH!!!

MASHA *lifts the nearest standing ashtray. She slings it mightily at the pay phone.*

CLERK *stops openmouthed in mid-tirade.* MASHA *repeats the action, going at it full tilt.*

*She busts the device clean off the wall and attacks it on the floor. Her fit worsens. She collapses, jerking, growling.*

OTHERS: Get her off the floor. Put her on a bench.

Get her lying down.

Get her sitting up!

Get something in between her jaws!

Don't let her bite!

SYLVESTER *enters from street door.*

SYLVESTER [*aside*]: There you are, you little magic thing! . . .

STAND ASIDE, PLEASE, DOCTOR COMING
    THROUGH.

GIVE WAY, THE DOCTOR'S IN THE HOUSE.

UH UH UH UH DOCTOR COMING THROUGH.

OTHERS: Thank goodness, Doctor. Hold her! Hold her!

She is strong!

Her spit is foaming like a case of rabies!

SYLVESTER: Nothing to alarm ourselves about.

CLERK: It's typical! It's standard stuff! It happens

All day long in here! It's par for the course!

SYLVESTER: Loosen her uh loosen her uh . . . clothing.

I deal with this stuff daily, too—the human

Body, human physique, the human form . . .
Did the patient make any predictions?
Often this variety of seizure
Takes them in a way they make predictions—
No? Perhaps you didn't recognize—
Uh sometimes they uh sometimes—Have a look
Now, at the racing form. Anything sound familiar?
Any of those names of horses there?

OTHERS: Missy, can you hear?
Somebody get some water—

SYLVESTER: I don't like uh I don't like to seem
Presumptuous, but I'm in charge here now.
Stand back and let me practice medicine!

BILL JENKS: Where's your bag?

SYLVESTER: My bag?

BILL JENKS: Your bag of tools.

SYLVESTER: My bag? Where am I, 1882?
I'm not a country doctor. I don't drive
A buggy through the daisies. That's a 'Vette
You'll see out there, you care to look, the blue
Corvette, the '98. And I paid cash.
And anyway we don't need implements.
We're not on the brink of surgery here.
A little air, a couple minutes' rest is all.
But I, myself, could use a little shot.
What're we sippin' behind the desk today?
Spare us an ounce or two, my boy, come on,
Don't balk—we understand, and we approve:
Only a natural monstrosity
Uh uh uh uh uh

Or penitential masochist endures
Eight hours in the Greyhound totally sober.

CLERK: I'm in agreement with you there! I quite agree!

SYLVESTER: Well—save a drop for company!
Can't have the citizens dispatched along
The routes by a comptroller in a state
A state of uh uh giddy inebri*ation*—
Who knows uh uh *how* things would uh! end up?

CLERK: They'd end up just exactly like they are,
With no one getting anywhere. Go on,
Kill it, sir, it's Everclear—
Seems like she's calmer—

JOHN:                                   Honey, just lay back.

SYLVESTER: Entranced and uncommunicative . . .

MASHA: LEMME DO THE HULA FOR YOU, BABY.

SYLVESTER: . . . She's fainted.

JOHN:                                   Doctor, why is her *voice* like that—

SYLVESTER: She's coming out of the physical part of it now.
We're entering the most important phase,
Prognostications, uh uh *sooth*saying—

BILL JENKS: Soothsaying? Buddy, what the hell is sooth?

SYLVESTER: We'll see a period of trancelike, "twilight
Semi-consciousness" we uh uh uh
Physicians like to call it, during which
—Does anybody have a racing form?
—I happen to have a racing form myself!
—I'm going to whisper names and races so
Our patient hears them in her twilight state
And then I think you'll uh uh be *intrigued*—

*Intrigued*, I say—all right, we've got the fifth
At Manor Downs. A lovely uh uh uh—
Outside of Austin there. They'll go the mile.
THE FIFTH AT MANOR DOWNS. THE FIFTH.
   Luke's Luck.
  Blue Streak, Destroyer, Dark Delight, Shazam.

MASHA: Idiot of ages!

SYLVESTER:         "Idiot—"
  Uh, no, the six: Shazam. Shazam, in fact,
  Is six, and number five is actually—

MASHA: Idiot idiot idiot! This one heals!

SYLVESTER: Settle down and pick me out a winner—

JOHN: This is William Jennings Bryan Jenks . . .

SYLVESTER: Jenks! The Shameful Shaman! Traveling?
  I do enjoy a Greyhound trip myself.
  It's magical. You get to *see* the country.

BILL JENKS: Who are you?

SYLVESTER:         I asked you first.

BILL JENKS:             I didn't hear you ask.

MASHA: SYLVESTER . . .

BILL JENKS:        O! Sylvester!—

SYLVESTER:            Uuh uh uh—

BILL JENKS: Sylvester's Big-As-Texas Topless Lounge!

SYLVESTER: Back off!—*Who is it now addresses me?*

MASHA: You know me.

SYLVESTER:      *Give me now predictions three.*

MASHA: Nothing for you.

SYLVESTER:       Nothing? Uh. Huh. Huh—

MASHA: You've let her go, you fool. She's found the healer.

SYLVESTER: This guy? uh uh uh—this guy's a fraud.

*Predictions three . . .*

MASHA: Get rid of him.

SYLVESTER: *Give me now predictions three.*

MASHA: Get rid of him, or I abide in silence.

SYLVESTER: Aw, come on, demon! Gimme couple *races*!

Look at the odds on uh uh Dark Destroyer!

. . . We're getting nothing here. [*To* BJ] You'll have to leave.

*Now*, please. You'll have to uh uh uh to leave—

BILL JENKS: Sucker, I been trying to leave all day.

You put me on a bus, I'll disappear.

JOHN: This is a *demon*, brother! You can *heal* her.

SYLVESTER: You are jinxin' my routine! Now blow!

GRANNY BLACK *wakes.*

GRANNY BLACK: Hot! Hot! Why do they say it's air-conditioned?

BILL JENKS: I wish I could nap as sound as you, young lady.

CLERK: Go grubbing on a grave all night;

Gnaw the dirt above a killer's corpse

While Huntsville lies in bed. Next day you'll nap.

GRANNY BLACK: I never grubbed on a grave! You slander me!

I think you're addled by the heat!

I think you're positively shatterpated!

MASHA: ARLENE.

GRANNY BLACK: Lonnie?

MASHA: ARLENE.

GRANNY BLACK: Is it . . . ? *Lonnie . . .*

MASHA: I'll see you tonight.

GRANNY BLACK: Lonnie . . .

MASHA: Sleep, sleep, Arlene. I'll see you tonight.

GRANNY BLACK: All right, Lonnie. Yes, my love . . .

SYLVESTER: My Lord.
  I've never seen her do like that. Uh . . . Uh . . .

BILL JENKS: DEMON! . . . DEMON! . . . DEMON! NAME
  YOURSELF!

MASHA: In whose name do you cast me out, Healer?

SYLVESTER: That's a damn good question. Who exactly
  Asked you to the party, anyway?
  In whose name do you cast out demons?

BILL JENKS: I cast out demons in my own damn name.

JOHN: That ain't gonna work.

BILL JENKS: You'll watch it work!

SYLVESTER: Now uh uh this disturbed young gal and I
  Have got a sort of system up and running,
  And your insertion of uh uh yourself
  Is absolutely unacceptable.

BILL JENKS: NAME YOURSELF!

SYLVESTER: JACKHAMMER!

BILL JENKS: . . . What?
  I beg your pardon? Demon name yourself?

SYLVESTER: Jackhammer Jake! I batter this man's throat.

SYLVESTER *howls and shakes.*

BILL JENKS: To tell the truth, I wasn't expecting this.
  Hold him down, John.—Don't let go of *her*!—
  Pry them jaws. Wider . . . Jackhammer Jake!

BJ *spits on his finger and touches it to* SYLVESTER*'s tongue.*

SYLVESTER: Uh uh uh uh uh uh uh uh

BILL JENKS: Jackhammer Jake!
  As Jesus promised in the Gospel of Mark
  That we shall cast out devils and lay healing

Touches on the sick, I touch you now!
Unloose the string on this man's tongue! Begone!
[SYLVESTER *calms*.]
. . . Now tell me, what did Peter Piper pick?
SYLVESTER: He picked your nose, you meddling piss, and I'd
Pay money to see him shove it up your hole . . .
Peter Piper picked a peck of pickled
Rubber baby buggy bumpers—wow.
This Mumble-Stumb's red-dogged my vocalize
From minute one. I had full-on, obscene
Tourette's till Mama whipped it out of me.
But let's just stop this tent revival here—
Before you get me past the point of cure
And on into the tongues and rattlesnakes.
You gotcher cookies. Come, girl, let's go home.
BILL JENKS: DEMON! NAME YOURSELF! *NOW!*
MASHA:                                        Dark
Delight.
Dark Delight at Manor Downs. Fifth race!
SYLVESTER: One down! All right, now, where's my sheet—
Back off now. Give her room. Give me my sheet!
I've lost my light—Don't you turn the lights on?
CLERK: Once in a while. But I never like what I see.
BILL JENKS: Let me do my work.
SYLVESTER:                          I need that demon!
MASHA *quakes at* BJ's *approach*.
JOHN: You can't expel a demon in the name
Of nothing but yourself—it's blasphemy.
BILL JENKS: Just let me take a whack at it. You'll see.

JOHN: It's blasphemy. The Bible's clear on that.
    Mark says, "In *my* name cast out devils."
BILL JENKS: Your good ol' brother Mark?
JOHN:                                        Come on!
BILL JENKS: All right, I will. I'll call on old JC.
    . . . Jesus Christ, they crucified you, huh?
    Holy Jesus, they crucified you good.
    Jesus Christ, they threw you in the pit
    And fed you meals of Spam and Wonder bread . . .
    But the crucifiers never ride the Greyhound.
    Jesus Christ . . .
    [*He falls to his knees.*]
                    It's Bill Jenks, fresh from prison.
    Been out half a day, and my report
    Says, Lord, it's still the world they killed you in.
    Says, Lord, the world is desperate and mean.
    Lord, come on now, turn an ear to me.
    Your Catholic priests are pederastic homos.
    Your preachers are sluts. They clutch your Book
    In one hand green from moneybags and poke
    Your Word with fingers reasty from young cunts.
    The sonsabitches crucify
    Occasionally a savior while revering
    Prophets their fathers lynched. The motherfuckers
    Live unchallenged, prosper, die unpunished.
    God, I hate them. Jesus hated them, too.
    Don't dispute me—Jesus Christ reviled them.
    He saw who held the hammer and the nails.
    He recognized who would and wouldn't hurt him,

And so he palled around with dwarfs and whores,

People everybody hated—tax collectors,

Lepers, urchins, strangers, widows, dummies . . .

Come on now, Jesus, turn an ear to me.

Jesus Christ, I am a criminal.

I am a tax collector, whore, and midget:

You have nothing to fear from the likes of me,

And nobody else in here is gonna hurt you,

For the crucifiers never ride the Greyhound.

Jesus Christ, I beg you for the power.

I beg you for the power and cry . . . DEMON!

[*He lays hands on* MASHA; *she writhes and screams.*]

DEMON, I BANISH YOU TO—

MASHA:                                    HEAR ME, HEALER!

. . . Spare me banishment to the pit of Hell,

But leave me to the world of things and men,

And I will grant you prophecies three.

SYLVESTER:                                YOU WHORE!

JOHN: Bill Jenks: Something good will come of this!

SYLVESTER: Masha—demon—buddy—talk to me—

MASHA: Only spare me the pit, and I will flee.

Spare me the pit, and I will prophesy . . .

BILL JENKS: . . . OK, I'll take the deal. No pit of Hell.

MASHA: Hand on the cross.

BILL JENKS:                          Hand on the cross. No pit.

Prophesy away, and walk the world

As long as men and things inhabit here.

SYLVESTER: He's got my damn predictions! I'm a pauper!

MASHA: Hear me, William Jennings Bryan Jenks:

I prophesy that you shall meet your mirror.

I prophesy that you shall raise the dead.
I prophesy one more: That like all men
William Jennings Bryan Jenks shall die,
And on his death an innocent shall be killed.
[BJ *lays his hands on her.*]
I FLEE!

JOHN:          . . . She's limp. That thing is gone.

SYLVESTER: Three predictions? That's your total score?
Three predictions worth exactly zero?
Son of a bitch. She could've made you wealthy
Ten times over. What a rube you are.
[*A siren; pulsing red and blue light that continues until*
*blackout.*]
Here comes the ambulance to the whore hospital.

BILL JENKS: I shall meet my mirror? I keep clear
Of mirrors. I don't like their face.
I guarantee I'll never raise the dead.
And naturally I'll die. But all the rest
Is nonsense. Let me see your racing form.
Maybe she's just handicapping horses.

CLERK [*holding radio*]: Hey there—John Cassandra—on the
news:
They set your mother's date an hour ago.
Isabel Cassandra: Death by poison!

JOHN *wails.*

   Lights narrow: GRANNY, *the cross, the sign:* SURPLUS STORE.
   HT *sings as he enters from Surplus Store.*

HT: *If you ever get to Houston*
      *Boy you better walk right*
      *You better not gamble*

*And you better not fight*
. . . What's all the fuss? Where'd everybody go?
Ma'am, I heard my friend I'm waiting on
Raising his voice in here. I know his voice.
GRANNY *wakes to see* HT *standing before the cross.*
GRANNY BLACK: Whose ghost are you? Which one? Which
   murdered angel?
HT: Do I look like a ghost? I'm not a ghost.
   (Am I a ghost? . . . I don't remember dying . . . )
   I'm waiting on a friend, a friend—I *know* his voice—
GRANNY BLACK: Harold Thomas Watson! I see you!
   I feel your fangs sinking into my soul!
   I didn't tell him to! Nobody told him!
   Demons sent and fetched him, slapped him, rocked
      him—
   Everybody knew he'd kill somebody.
   *I'm* the one he should have killed—he loved me!
   *I'm* the one he should have killed—I loved him!
   I swear I'm leaving town. I'm bound for Dallas.
   I won't be here among your children nor
   Your children's children on the Huntsville streets—
   They'll never have to look at me again!
   Leave this poor old woman to the black
   And miserable damnation love has earned her.
*Her wailing blends with ambulance's siren.*

BLACKOUT

# PART II

*About a year later.*

*Split scene: Left, hospital waiting room. Right, hospital room.*

*Lights up stage right:*

*Hospital room. Early summer morning. Dark but for the light of the monitors, and a bit of dawn.*

SIMON *lies in bed, a silhouette.*

SIMON: I have kissed your prayers kissed your prayers
    Roller coaster rollin' through the rain
    The oceanic shoulders of the throng
    Undulating slowly breakfastward
    Mobile tit!

NURSE *has entered. She opens the window.*

NURSE:         A lovely one is coming!
    Lovely! I'll just crack the jamb before
    The hot of the day, so's you can breathe the morning.
    . . . O, Lordy God, it smells so sweet and green
    It almost nearly stinks.

SIMON:                    Soft fuck-me music
    Plays the little baby radio
    Bare room shaken by a passing train

NURSE: The little baby radio. That's cute.

*She turns on radio. While she fluffs his pillows, records his vitals, etc.:*

JIMMY BOGGS [*sings on radio*]:
>    All your promises
>    The things you said

NURSE: That Jimmy Boggs is just untalented.

JIMMY BOGGS [*sings on radio*]:
>    Using grand words
>    Like eternity and love

NURSE: A singing voice like garbage cans turned over.

*She cuts the radio.*

SIMON: Your holy pussy your precious cunt
>    There's never been a sweeter ride to Hell

NURSE: How quiet and *delicious* is the air.
>    Like anything can happen in the world.
>    What an atmosphere . . . Ah, God. Ah, God . . .
>    They mow the lawns, it drags me back to Dallas . . .
>    I wish they had the ice-cream trucks again . . .

*Meanwhile,* WILL BLAINE *has entered in medical smock.*

WILL: You wish they had the ice-cream trucks again.

SIMON: The generous wide feet of pachyderms

NURSE: We're almost done here, Doc.

WILL:                                      I'm not a doctor.
>    Just a tech.

NURSE:              Blood?

WILL:                       In a sense.

NURSE:                                Let's see—

SIMON: Geezing bugspray in the slimy night

NURSE: —Do you have orders? I don't seem to have—

WILL: Uh—no. I'm not your colleague. Actually,
     Simon is my brother.
NURSE:                    Simon's brother!
     But it's a little early, don't you think?
     Official hours—
WILL:                    I drove down from work.
     Been floating on that road since midnight, after
     the post-injection wrap-up drinks at Mursky's
     Bar and Grill but definitely mostly Bar,
     Drifting through the general emptiness
     From Huntsville: Seven hours in the rain
     and more than slightly drunk, and I saw never
     A single car. Or house. Or tree. Or star.
NURSE: O well, that's Texas! It's a long old ways
     Between and not a whole lot when you get there . . .
     My niece got married to a Huntsville man.
WILL: I'm over at the Unit. At the Walls.
NURSE: The Walls?
WILL:          The prison?
NURSE:                    O. The prison? O!
     They executed someone there last night!—
     Some crazy feller killed his wife and all
     His little children . . . Well, my niece's husband
     Thomas Hill works at the Walls. I guess
     He goes around confusing people, too,
     Looking like the uniform of something else.
     . . . Well now, since you're a tech, you're probably . . .
     There's things to do the *fam*ily might not . . .
     We like to avoid unsightly *sights*—

WILL:                               The bag.

NURSE: I'm gonna change the bag, and such.

WILL:                               OK.

NURSE: His little children! God Himself can't tell you
        Why that feller killed them. Well, he did,
        And now it's eye for eye and tooth for tooth.
        They strapped him to the slab and—life for life.

WILL: I'd say that's pretty much it, in a nutshell,
        That's what we do.

NURSE:                     You do? *You* do? Do *you*?

WILL: With his last breath he proclaimed his innocence.

SIMON: A whitetail deer goes walking past in the rain
        A dream of volcanoes rides past on a train
        A spider crouched alive betwixt her lungs

NURSE: I'm sorry; but it stops him—

WILL:                               When you yank
        His crotch a couple yanks, it shuts him up?

NURSE: Manipulation of the scrotal—*well*—
        I know! The whole world's highly entertained!
        He's quite a favorite hereabouts. A team
        From Dallas, on the first of every month,
        Descends upon us, specialists from Dallas—

WILL: How about that!—lining up to plunk
        The magic twanger of my brother's scrotum!
        My helpless brother's balls! Nurse . . . Vandermere:
        I'm not here visiting the vegetable.
        This thing they're gonna do—I'm here for that.

NURSE: What—thing?

WILL:                 Wal now I don' perzackly know.
        I would assume the staff would know.

NURSE:                                    The staff?

WILL: The personnel employed here. Such as you.

NURSE: I don't know *any*thing about a *thing*.

WILL: A medical procedure, I presume,
        At which, for reasons they have not explained,
        They want the whole damn family to assemble.

NURSE: But . . . nothing's scheduled . . .

WILL:                                    Nothing.

NURSE:                                    Not a thing.

WILL: The vegetable's entire day is free.

NURSE: What you don't seem to realize is a coma
        Doesn't make them deaf. They hear us talk,
        They understand, and Simon knows what's what.

WILL: You claim the calabash is cognizant.

NURSE: If *I* was being visited by you,
        And *I* was in a coma—I would die!

WILL: I think— Is that my sister-in-law out there?

NURSE: I'd slip on out to sea and sail away.

WILL: It is. Ah, God!—the other one! *Her* sister!
        What's this all about?

SIMON:                          Who owns the rain

NURSE: It doesn't take a death grip!

WILL:                                Like he cares!
        He didn't even blink. He kinda sorta
        Rolls his eyes around though, doesn't he.
        A six-foot-long Señor Potato-Head . . .
        And not one blister, huh? Not one hair singed.
        That's what ya git fer smokin'!—might as well
        Be ashes, huh?

NURSE:                  He got like this from smoking?

WILL: Not exactly smoking—breathing smoke,
       Smoke inhalation. Very bad for you.
SIMON: I would kiss you even if it killed me
*Meanwhile,* JAN *and* STACY *have entered.*
JAN: Let him a-*lone*!
WILL:                 It shuts him up, or so
       I'm told—and as we've just been demonstrating.
SIMON: Even if it killed me I would kiss you
JAN: Simon, hon? . . . I think he's glad to see me!
STACY: Simon? Can he hear? His *voice* is all—
SIMON: Kuala Lumpur Kuala Lumpur Kuala
       Lumpur
JAN:              See! He knows Ko-ala Lumpur!
STACY: All those voices, all those different—Jan,
       I never heard those voices before.
       Did you ever hear those voices before?
NURSE: Visiting hours haven't really *started*—
STACY: He's like a boombox on a merry-go-round!
WILL: This is Simon's wife, my sister-in-law—
JAN: Jan.
NURSE:  I'm pleased to meet you.
JAN:                             This is Stacy,
       *Simon's* sister-in-law, which is because
       I'm Simon's wife, and she's my sister— Calling
       Koala Lumpur! Simon!
STACY:                      Can he hear?
JAN: Are you receiving, Simon?
WILL:                          No. He's not.
STACY: He talked right *to* us!—He was buying gold
       In Koala Lumpur when the fire struck

That shopping mall and pumped it full of smoke
And choked him till he got like this! Now, Simon,
Form your thoughts, take all the time you want,
Visiting hours haven't even started—
WILL: He isn't "forming" any "thoughts." All right:
You're here; he's here; everybody's here.
Now how about a little explanation?
JAN: Well! The lights came on!
NURSE:                     It's eight a.m.
It's still a half an hour till *official*—
WILL: And not "Koala." K-*U*-A-L-A—
JAN: He was buying *gold*, he was *investing*—
Tragedy strikes us anytime it wants,
Even in places like Koala Lumpur—
STACY: *Kua*-la Lumpur, *Kua*-la Lumpur, Jan—
JAN: —No matter what you try to call yourself!
You can't escape life even by pretending!
*Meanwhile, the* DOCTOR *has entered.*
DOC: So, Simon draws a crowd!
NURSE:                 They jumped the gun
A couple minutes, Doc—
DOC:                 Good morning, all!
SIMON: I have a dog who is a lilac bush
JAN: We *have* a dog who is a lilac bush!
SIMON: Kuala Lumpur Kuala . . . Kuala . . . Kuala . . .
STACY: Lumpur—Lumpur—*Lumpur*, Simon, *Lumpur*!
JAN: But, see, our dog is *buried* by the lilac!
We always say he's turned in*to* the lilac!
So, Doctor, when he says I have a *dog*,
He's talking about our actual *universe*,

And an *act*ual dog, also an actual *lilac*.
And even if we don't have a koala bear,
There actually *are* koala bears in China,
Or over there where Kuala Lumpur is.
DOC: . . . Mind is the only actuality.
*Breakfast chimes sound.*
STACY: O, Doctor . . . Nasum? That is so . . . pro-*found*.
Like what if this life isn't really real?
DOC: And what if we're like Simon, in a realm
We can't imagine, in a spastic coma—
STACY: A hospital in some enchanted dream,
A magic hospital . . . A "spastic coma"?
DOC: What life we truly live we'll never know.
The only hope we have is to assume
That what we see is where we are . . .
STACY:                                    Doctor,
Why does Simon jabber like a zoo?
DOC: The human brain, the . . . May I know your name?
STACY: Forgive me: Stacy Daley Morgan Blaine.
But I should drop the Blaine, as I'm divorced—
Again! But then, I didn't drop the Morgan—
DOC: Now, isn't "Blaine"—? Now, Simon, *you're* a Blaine—
STACY: Well, I was married to him, first. He gets around.
DOC: In rather a tiny circle!
WILL:                         He's a sucker:
Snoring in the kingdom of the vegetables
He ain't a whole lot dumber than he was.
DOC: I see, and, Stacy, that makes you the patient's—?
STACY: Former wife and current sister-in-law.
I'm sure you know my sister, Jan—

DOC:                                    Of course.
        A real Penelope!—
STACY:                        And Will, our brother-in-law—
        Jan's former brother-in-law, but now her current,
        And currently my former brother-in-law.
DOC: Pleased to meet you, Will. And, Stacy: *charmed*
        And *very* pleased.
STACY:                        The feeling's . . . *mutual* . . .
SIMON: I sound like I'm shrinking
STACY:                            —And! A "spastic
        coma"?
DOC: The injury to Simon's synapses,
        The anaerobic outrage to his brain,
        The shock of oxygen starvation on
        A mystery so frail as the electric
        Pilgrimage an impulse undertakes
        Along a route of stimulated nerves
        Has induced in Simon Blaine a wild condition,
        A hyperactive, vegetative state,
        A chronic, spastic, comatose condition
        Marked by baffling random episodes
        Apparently the property of the dark
        And chiefly somnolent prefrontal lobes:
        Pseudo-verbal, faux-autistic, splashed
        With flowery jets and startling and bright
        Ejaculations with aphasic overtones.
STACY: Overtones . . . and episodes . . . I see . . .
DOC:  He reads out almost epileptic when
        We hook him to the EEG. And so . . .
STACY: He has these fits.

DOC:                          And so he has these fits.
         —A rare and baffling form of coma.
JAN:                                    *Rare?*
         There's never been another coma like it!
STACY: And nothing can be done?
DOC:                          A case like this,
         We offer consolation. Never hope.
JAN: But you're not *God*.
DOC:                          And I don't claim to be.
JAN: But he's right there! Right *here*!—Simon!
         Wife to Simon! What are you thinking, Simon—
         I wish I could join him there. I struggle to get there.
         But how do you struggle? I struggle with my heart,
         My soul. I make an effort in my chest.
         With my love, my force of love.—It's bullshit!
         He's there and I'm here. What are you thinking? . . .
         TELL ME! TELL ME! RE-TARD! WRETCH!
             *TELL ME!*
DOC: Nurse!
NURSE:      Ma'am! No!
WILL:                 Jan, *stop* it!
STACY:                                 Stop it, Jan!
         [*A brief struggle.*]
         Stop it, stop it, stop it, stop it! STOP!
         . . . There are comas and there are comas, Jan.
         This is one of those. The kind the very
         Wisest doctors cannot comprehend.
         So let's stop beating around the bush, OK?
         Your husband isn't ever coming home.
         This spastic coma person isn't Simon,

'Cause Simon's off in Coma-Simon-Land
Married to a Spastic Coma Girl.
He doesn't hear a single word we say.
He doesn't, and he didn't, and he won't.
So no more sex. Just learn to masturbate.
—O, well! I'm sorry! I don't make the rules!

WILL: Will someone give this stupid bitch a shot
And put us all out of our misery?

STACY: You wish you had your little death machine?

WILL: You bet your plastic boobs.

DOC:                                        Now—now—now—now—

STACY: *You're* the reason I divorced him, Will—
When we were living in North Houston, Will—
I don't forget who introduced him to
Sylvester's Big-As-Texas Topless Lounge—

JAN: I wouldn't be caught dead inside that place!

STACY: You've always been a rotten influence—

JAN: In there it's all black light and fuzzy dice!

DOC: Ah, me!—it's difficult to make a point
In these surroundings. Why don't we adjourn—

WILL: No. What procedure have you scheduled here?

DOC: Excuse me. Was there something scheduled?

WILL:                                        Yes!
I drove all night from Huntsville to attend—
To what were you referring, Jan? You claimed
Some bold experiment was taking place—

DOC: Have we experiments on the agenda, Nurse?

NURSE: Not from now till three p.m.—No, sir!

JAN: 'Cause all *you* know to do is grab his pecker!
Experiments won't save him! He needs faith!

*You* saw the pictures on TV, *you* watched
The faces of those red-hot, burning people—
Like faces in a painting, witnessing
Their resurrection in a revelation,
Riding escalators toward the flames
Like souls ascending toward Atomic Heaven—
STACY: Or Hell! Pockets of Hell! Of Hell!—I mean,
Subterranean shopping center fires
Are breaking out all over God's green earth.
It's punishment for something—*you* know what:
Divorce, and dope, and gambling; lesbians,
Teenage sexpot prostitution rings,
Child-molester grandmas, *Mardi* Gras—
WILL: What the hell full name is Stacy short for?
STACY: It's not. I'm only Stacy, *ma chérie*!
WILL: And *now* what? What are *these* fools up to
Out the window here? Will someone promise me
My family is not a party to
This further nonsense in the parking lot?
Here we have a maniac with a cross,
I mean it's big, this sucker's big enough
To mount a dolphin on, he's standing there
Beside it like he's posing for a photo—
Looking stupid, I don't have to add—
And, am I psychic? Why am I so *sure*
That these two *other* maniacs are coming *here*?
JAN: That's William Jennings Bryan Jenks, the healer.
WILL: A heeler. What is that? A person?
JAN:                                                         Yes,
A healer is a person.

WILL:                    There are dogs
    Called blue heelers—fact my neighbor has one.
    Had one, I should say. It's dead. It drowned.
MASHA *and* BILL JENKS *enter, both in quite conservative garb,*
MASHA *in gray,* BJ *in black.* BJ*'s hair has grown out; he wears it*
*swept back in a shining pompadour.*
BILL JENKS: Where's this drowning victim?
    . . . This is the man who drowned?
STACY: Nobody drowned him. He was in a fire.
BILL JENKS: Is this a burn unit?
NURSE:                    Perpetual Care.
    He wasn't burned.
BILL JENKS:              The fire didn't burn him?
STACY: More like he suffocated in the smoke,
    Which you could almost say the fire drowned him—
WILL: Coincidence, here—I was telling how
    My neighbor's dog got drowned last Sunday morning.
    Nobody home, he went and jumped right in
    The swimming pool and couldn't clamber out.
    Hung on—hung on—hung on till noon, almost—
    Gave up; went under; drowned.
BILL JENKS:                          How do they know?
WILL: They don't. I do. I let it drown. I watched,
    Sipping a Bloody Mary on a Sunday morn.
    The rest of God's creation was at church.
    Sunday morning; drinking alone: I love it.
    I don't like heelers.
WILL *and* BJ *stand, each facing the other, as in a mirror.*
BILL JENKS:              Are you copying me?
WILL: Are you copying me?

BILL JENKS:                    Cut it out.

WILL:                                    Cut it out.

BILL JENKS: All I have to do is remain silent.

     . . . Well, aren't you going to copy that?

WILL: Aren't you going to copy that?

BILL JENKS:                              You win.

WILL: You lose.

MASHA:              Brother, we're in danger.

WILL:                                    Will Blaine . . .

BILL JENKS: Bill Jenks.

STACY:                    Well! *Bill* and *Will*! Could be

     You guys are twins! Twins torn apart at birth—

SIMON: Watch me jack off with my solar flare

STACY: Simon Blaine, hush! You've got company!

MASHA: The lesser demons bow to something here.

     Satan's pouring honey down my spine.

BILL JENKS: Satan can't be everywhere at once,

     And right now he's in Hollywood or Vegas.

WILL: Who publishes the diabolical

     Itinerary? There a cable channel?

BILL JENKS: He gravitates toward Sodom and Gomorrah.

WILL: Really.

BILL JENKS: Sure. The old boy craves a little

     Action same as everybody else.

WILL: Was it *Twenty-Twenty*? Or *Sixty Minutes*?

     I thought they made a worldwide fool of you.

     —OK, it's rude of me to say so, sorry—

     What'd you call your outfit there in Dallas,

     Church of the Holy Sacred Bank Account?

     Ripped of your congregation, shot a guy,

Landed up in Huntsville, where I work:
I bet I've seen you, out there in the fields
Hacking with a hoe (—excuse me, ma'am!),
Slaving away with black-eyed Susans winkin'
And stinkin' like a Dallas trollop (—'scuse me!);
Suspected dealer, quantity cocaine—

BILL JENKS: O yeah, I shot a man. He didn't die.
I get the chance again—who knows?

WILL: You'd think a guy would sense his status!— Yeah,
They had you on with Ron the Levitator
And that frog-voice freak transvestite with a lisp
Driving his spangled automatic wheelchair,
Jimmy—

NURSE:　　　　Boggs! "The Singer of the South"!
You oughta heal his *singing*!

BILL JENKS:　　　　　　　　There are limits.

WILL: I have to say, he does look like he's healed.
Healed by whom, by use of which powers,
I couldn't guess. Or even healed of what.
But, anyway, he's acting different now.

BILL JENKS: That's right. He ran a marathon last month.

WILL: That's right. He came in way behind the pack.

BILL JENKS: That's right, and running on two legs. His
spangled
Wheelchair graces our museum now.

WILL: They mentioned that— You have your own museum!

BILL JENKS: Most of one. Construction's under way.

WILL: Construction's stalled, according to *Sixty Minutes*,
Stalled while the IRS and FTC
Shine a light on your money.

BILL JENKS:                         Let it shine,
    There ain't a lot to see.

WILL:                           You claim you're clean.

BILL JENKS: Nope. I just claim there isn't any money.

SIMON: THERE'S NEVER BEEN A SWEETER RIDE TO
    HELL

BILL JENKS: This one's getting agitated now.

STACY: I take it you're a husband-and-wife team?

BILL JENKS: We are as siblings.

WILL:                         Ooh, you two are *juicy*.

SIMON: I'll climb back up your cunt and suck your mind
    The way we used to do when we were lovers

JAN: Simon! Shame on you!

STACY:                       Well, talk about a mouth!

BILL JENKS: You recognize him, don't you? Yes. You do.

MASHA: It's him. It's him.

STACY:                       Do you *eat* with that mouth?

DOC: Actually, he's nourished through this tube.

MASHA: I'm free of you! You hear? Leave me alone!

WILL: Just grab his scrotum there to shut him up.
    Just reach on out—go on—and shake the hand
    Of the old banana, with a manly grip.

NURSE: Doctor Nasum, please, this doesn't seem—

WILL: Take hold! There can't be any harm in it,
    Right? Big deal, as far as he's concerned . . .
    I used to get him down and drool a strand—
    Now this'll git 'im, if he's there a-tall—
    And slurp it back—

NURSE:                       Now, what on *earth*!—

WILL:                                 Aha!

STACY: You can't spit in a coma person's face!

WILL: You get a pain response? Huh, buddy? There!

NURSE: For goodness' sakes alive, he's *hurting* him!

*They restrain him,* DOC *and* NURSE *taking either arm.*

WILL: The point is that I'm *not*. He doesn't hurt.
But everybody else—this family,
Our parents, this man's wife, his wife's relations—
Het up by this fireball of faith,
Yinked and yanked by hope in God like gobs
Of spit he dangles from his fat, red mouth—
His doctor shouldn't let them play these games.
I want this sucker ceremony canceled!
Who is actually in attendance here?

NURSE: It's Dr. Cassady. He makes his rounds
Just after lunch on weekdays, Sir.

WILL: Then page old Hopalong immediately.
Come on! —He doesn't want to see his patient
Used like bait to fish for dollars, does he?

SIMON: LET IT THUNDER FARTS AND RAIN DOWN
VOMIT

JAN: STACY!

STACY [*grabbing* SIMON's *crotch*]: Hon, it's simple courtesy.

MASHA: He's wild for me. The demon's wild for me.

WILL: Jesus Christ, Morticia—lighten up!

BILL JENKS: I'd like to be alone with Simon now.

WILL: Go right ahead. Remember—manly grip!

DOC *and* NURSE *begin dragging* WILL *out.*

BILL JENKS: No— Let him stay. I want him here. Let go.

DOC: If *I* were Simon's primary physician—

BILL JENKS: Go on, the rest of you. Leave us alone.

[*To* MASHA] You especially. We can't have you here.
*All exit.* BJ *alone with* WILL *and* SIMON. WILL *collects himself,*
*goes to window.*

WILL: What's he saying? . . . (Jesus. What a morning . . . )

       Sights . . . heights . . . Keep your eyes—the prize—

BILL JENKS: Keep your sights

       On the heights

       Keep your eyes

WILL:                On the prize. The guy's a public nuisance.

BILL JENKS: He's with me.

WILL:                He would be, wouldn't he?

       . . . I'm calmer now.

BILL JENKS:         No need to apologize.

WILL: I feel no need. I'm not apologizing.

       My position hasn't altered; I'm just calmer.

       Simon, too.

BILL JENKS:      I don't expect you like this

       Invasion of your realm—

WILL:               It ain't my realm.

       I'm not a doctor. I'm just Simon's brother.

BILL JENKS: I thought you were a medical man.

WILL:                    I am.

BILL JENKS: Then please don't be so hostile. I don't go

       So far as to suggest you look on us

       As colleagues, but I think we share a goal.

WILL: I'm a technician of a very special kind.

       I don't fix people. Quite the opposite.

       I supervise the termination teams.

BILL JENKS: Sounds like you're in the personnel division.

WILL: No. —The tie-down team, the I-V team . . .

BILL JENKS:                                              I see.

WILL: Next to me, boys, Lucifer never fell.

BILL JENKS: You execute the folks.

WILL:                                         That's not quite true.
    We execute the sentence, not the person.

BILL JENKS: And who, exactly, executes the person?

WILL: "To execute" means "to carry out."
    Well, I guess in the end we carry them out.
    . . . So you do the opposite of what I do.

BILL JENKS: I've never raised the dead.

WILL:                                         But—in a sense.

BILL JENKS: I've never raised the dead.

WILL:                                    Why don't you try?
    Go where the dead go. Haunt the mortuaries.
    Give 'em the razzle-dazzle of your gift
    And see if anybody cheats the grave . . .
    —What's the matter with him now? My God!

BILL JENKS: The demon's agitated. SETTLE DOWN!
    . . . I wonder where you know my assistant from?

WILL: Morticia? Man, I've seen that honey shake
    Her titties! You a preacher, or a pimp?

BILL JENKS: The line between the two is faint. I think
    It moves. I've found myself on either side.

WILL: You didn't move yourself?

BILL JENKS:                          Not to my knowledge . . .
    Maybe . . . If I moved, I didn't feel it . . .
    Well, I just had to ask. Not my affair,
    But I was curious. Now you can leave.

WILL: You think you're safe alone? I mean, he's strong—

He may be out of it, but—

BILL JENKS:                               I'll be fine.

WILL: The Lord protects you.

BILL JENKS:                         I believe he does.

WILL: You trust in the Lord.

BILL JENKS:                       I find him predictable . . .

We've got three this week. Uh. Tuesday, Wednesday,

I think Thursday . . . Thursday?

WILL:                                    So do we.

BILL JENKS: Yes, three . . . Three executions in three days?

WILL: Hey, I don't make the reservations, boys.

I just fly the plane.

BILL JENKS:                   Here and yonder,

Even in prison, I've met up with good

And decent people. But . . . How do you say this? . . .

I've never met one in the mirror.

WILL:                             . . . Yeah . . .

O well, that's life, huh?

BILL JENKS:                   That's life on Death Row.

WILL: I don't get you. Do you believe, or not?

Do you really heal? And cleanse these souls

Of maladies and spirits? Do you care?

BILL JENKS: The gift is real, but I just turn a buck.

I turn a buck, he executes his vague

Intentions on a baffled universe:

Win-win . . . Of course, he screws with me.

That's his style—the gift, and then the gag.

And in return I fail to reverence him,

Fail in gratitude. I fail to love him.

WILL: Wow! You *are* an existentialist.
It's a little hard to see that message landing
Anywhere. It's no surprise you're bankrupt.
BILL JENKS: Aah, they're just watching television, man.
I tell it like I see it, but I doubt
There's anybody listening. Faith is scary.
Faith affords its consolations, sure—
By opening the maw to the dark depths
Where going blind and getting lost and hurt
Seem understandable and natural,
And all night long two graces fall like rain:
A tragic sense of life, and hope of Heaven.
WILL: Are grace and Heaven all you've got to offer?
Man, I've watched one hundred twenty people
Die because I killed them with a button.
I've seen them breathe their last—the air
Goes out, and out, and then they kind of shiver
And there's this second where you know it's over
And it ain't never gonna start again.
. . . On summer evenings I sit on my porch
And listen to this train that comes along.
I listen to the wheels bang on the tracks,
I listen to the whistle drag the air
And fill the world, and fade, and leave it empty,
And I am gonna tell you: Heaven never
Dreamt of anything as sweet as that:
To listen to a train and not be dead.
VOICE ON RADIO: Insects are often the only witnesses
To a crime.
BILL JENKS [*to* SIMON]: Did you turn that thing on?

WILL: It wasn't me.

BILL JENKS: Well turn the damn thing off.

VOICE ON RADIO: The president's order has been disobeyed. *Soft music on radio . . .*

BILL JENKS: All right. It's time you left us, please.

WILL: Don't *heal*, or even *touch*, or even *think*
About— Don't—don't . . . Don't hurt him. He's my
brother.

BILL JENKS: . . . No. I wouldn't hurt him, Mr. Blaine.

WILL *exits.*

> BILL JENKS *falls and weeps.*

> VOICE ON RADIO *laughs hysterically*—SIMON *joins in.*

BILL JENKS *quells them with a laying on of hands.*

SIMON: HEALER! . . . HEALER, NOLI MI TANGERE!

BILL JENKS: All right. They're gone. I'm here. Who are you,
demon?

SIMON: Et cetera non sequitur mon cher

BILL JENKS: Is it you? Are you the same one?

SIMON: E pluribus non sequitur tyrannis

BILL JENKS: I saw this movie. Everybody saw it.

Are you the demon who prophesies, or not?

SIMON: O. This. Yes. That.
Jack
Sprat
Begat Jehosephat.

BILL JENKS: Cut it out. Get serious. You know
I coulda had your ass in Huntsville—
Coulda sent you to the Pit. You owe me.

SIMON: Coulda shoulda woulda hadda oughta.

BILL JENKS: God! There's something *wrong* with me or
     something.
     There's something wrong with me or something wrong
     With money. Anyhow, we tangle wrong,
     Me and the dollar . . . What a mess, what . . . All
     Those people on the money—can't they see me?
SIMON: I love you. Love you with a love that burns.
BILL JENKS: If I'da lived a hundred years ago,
     I'd be riding circuit, I'd be praising God
     And healing hearts and saving souls
     And money'd never touch me long enough
     To suck itself inside me like it has.
SIMON: I love you with a love that burns and smokes.
BILL JENKS: OK, OK, you're probably aware
     We've got a hearing set for Wednesday next
     To go and file for Chapter—I don't know—
     Eleven, Thirteen, Twenty-one—they make
     The whole thing sound like Vegas, don't they?
     They tap you out as quick as Vegas, too.
     But you know me: I'll bet my shorts and socks
     And get back in the game, or hitchhike home
     As naked as my mama made me. Anyhow,
     The institute is broke, but the foundation
     Holds several thousand shares of Motorola.
     Here's the thing: This Freddie Spendersnap,
     The NASCAR racer, wants to make a swap,
     My Motorola for a razor-thin
     Controlling interest in his hot-dog thing,
     His vending franchise thing. It sounds superb,

It's very liquid, totally set up—
I mean, you figure hot dogs are forever—
But Motorola's flirting with Verizon,
The big fat cell-phone company; O, yeah,
Verizon makes my Motorola pretty—
But if the feds resolve to yank tobacco
Sponsorship of NASCAR, man, the brokest
Sucker in the South is gonna be
The guy with fifteen hundred red-and-white
Stripèd hats and fifteen hundred hot-dog carts.
*But*. Cell phones give you cancer. They could tank.
SIMON: "Spendersnap." I think you made that up.
BILL JENKS: . . . Why can't I be like simple John and stand
My cross in a melting Texas parking lot—
What did he have to endure to get like that?
Remove from me these bonds of self . . . Release . . .
Shit. Am I praying to you? Praying to a demon?
SIMON: Jenks, I reject your terminology.
*Demon* is a term whose definition
Seems to shift its shape as much as we do.
Call me a teenymeanymotherfucker.
BILL JENKS: . . . So . . . am I Motorola, or Freddie's Franks?


BLACKOUT


*Lights up stage left:*
*Hospital waiting room.* MASHA *at the window.*
WILL *enters. Comes up close behind her.*
WILL: Look at this guy. Just can't wait to give
His life away. He's chomping at the bit.

He's straining at the traces. Giddyap,
Ol' hoss. Drag that contraption into
The third millennium. You get farther and farther
From Calvary all the time. Farther and farther
From the place of skulls. Farther from Golgotha.
. . . An overpowering scent of blossoms on
The air today. Inebriating.

MASHA:                           Just about a stench.

WILL: Or is it your perfume?

MASHA:                     I wear no scent.

WILL: But I can smell you. You smell womanly.
My my, you give a man an appetite.
You're womanly. Dazzlingly. Deeply.

MASHA: I don't hear such talk. It strikes me deaf.

WILL: I know you from Sylvester's. I know you
From head to toe three nights a week stark naked,
No matter how you cover up in gray.
I don't forget the times I watched you dance.
First time, I said to my buddies, Hey now, there's
The type I crave, a dancing contradiction:
I crave my women simultaneously
Loose and tight.

MASHA:                   You're talking to the walls.
You're talking to the moon. Nobody hears you.

WILL: You cast one glance and liquefied my bones
And alla that. Sweet Jesus, what a rack.
What a set of pins.

MASHA:                   Would you not swear?

WILL: "A set of pins"?

MASHA:             You took the Lord in vain.

WILL: I'll take him any way that I can get him,
Honey baby lover fucker-doll.

MASHA: . . . Who's the ones with everything stripped off?
Who's the peep show? Is it really me?
I strut along and toss down feed to you.
You hunch there with your glass of screw-top wine
And all the feelings naked in your face.
You gobble me down with your eyes, but you don't see
me.
You see the act, you see your fantasy
And not the person working at a job.
You see me panting for you, but I'm bored,
My ankles hurt, my car got repossessed,
I'd like to move because my rickety
Apartment's on the building's sunny side—
The prancing slut is prancing in your head.
You got me backwards. I'm not undercover.
I never was so hidden as when I was naked.
. . . And plus fact is I ain't no Norma Jean.
I'm sort of regular, with decent legs.
Dim light, I'm gorgeous.

WILL:                                        Dancing decent legs.
Decent legs made for indecent dancing.

MASHA: I think I wish to stop this conversation.

WILL: Dim light, spilt liquor, dancing decent legs.
. . . Where does he keep you stashed?

MASHA: In Hawk Hills. Outside Fort Worth. Way outside.

WILL: I think you need to get to Houston.

MASHA:                                        No.

WILL: But not downtown. Just out there by the lake.
     I'd put you by the golf course. Weekend nights
     We head downtown, see what the action's like.
MASHA: I don't like the city. I never did.
     It smells. It stinks. I mean it reeks.
WILL: The smells and lights and noise and all the tense
     Faces and the cries of the lunatics.
     You've gotta get out of Hawk Hills, swoop down
     To Second Street and put the world before you.
     Downtown. In the night. That's where you hide.
     Do you know what this is?
MASHA:                     Money, yeah. So what?
WILL: Two dollars.
MASHA:        Stick it up your ass!
WILL:                  Come on.
     You never took a little nap for money?
MASHA: You can go to Hell!
WILL:                 I'll take you with me!
     . . . All I did was watch. Not like the others.
     Everybody knows what goes on there.
     "They dance till two and then they screw." That's
       right.
     Sylvester pimped you as a nightly thing.
     You sucked and blew and bent and spread and squirmed
     For college jocks and gap-tooth farmer boys
     And fat-ass salesmen in their Cadillacs.
     You gave each other phony names and fucked,
     And they were all your dirty little husbands,
     And Jesus Christ can strike me down and turn

My guts to pus if I've said one false thing.
Look me in the face and tell me Jesus
Jack is gonna cancel who you are.
      . . . Baby . . . You are suckin' my cock with your eyes.
MASHA: Don't. Don't. I'm bad luck. It's just gonna hurt you.
WILL: I would kiss you even if it killed me.
      . . . Jesus won't protect you. Hell with him.
You wanna hide? You wanna leave yourself?
You need a stack of credit cards, a beauty parlor,
Stocks and bonds and money in the bank,
A little sports car and a big suburban wagon,
Air-conditioned condo by the golf course,
Fifty inches on your television.
Jesus isn't gonna give you that.
I'm the one who's gonna give you that.
My fingerprints on your velour.

MASHA:                                        O, stop.

WILL: I'm gonna lift your skirt.
MASHA: You can lift it a little bit.
WILL: I'm gonna lift it higher.
MASHA: You can lift it a little higher.
WILL: I'm gonna lift it all the way up. Do you want me to?
MASHA: You can. OK. You can if you want to.
WILL: I'm gonna do whatever I want.
MASHA: I know you are. OK. I know you are.


BLACKOUT


*Lights up stage right:*
BJ *and* SIMON *as before.*

SIMON: I love this guy. You're such a baby loser!

      You shit yer pants while pissing on yer shoes.

BILL JENKS: You owe me, bud. I left you free to wander.

      Didn't I leave you free for fun and travel?

      Haven't you had some share of fun and travel?

SIMON: Of course I have! —This year or so, since Huntsville,

      I've circuited the earth a dozen times,

      Entering any soul who offered entrance.

      From sin to sin I've wafted like a spore.

      I've bent the gambler to his knee,

      I've dragged the junkie through the grime,

      I've parked the harlot on her corner,

      I've sent the rapist on his round.

      I've given reasons to the traitor,

      Glossy varnish to the liar,

      Piety to hypocrites—

      And left them hobbled and alone,

      Waiting like dogs for any scent of me.

      And next, who knows? Some other galaxy.

      Prepare for takeoff! Five, four, three, two, one . . .

      *In whose name do you cast out spirits, Healer?*

BILL JENKS: I'm not casting anybody out.

      We're talking here. We're making simple average

      Conversation as we grope toward

      An understanding.

SIMON:              Or you cast me out.

BILL JENKS: I could. I could. So why not demonstrate

      A modicum of flexibility—

      On both our parts? I let you play with Simon;

      You hand me out my standard three predictions.

SIMON: You've had your three. And one just now came true.
    Today you met your mirror, as I'm sure
    You gather. Sometime soon you'll touch a corpse's
    Clay and set it throbbing on the slab,
    And when, one day, as all men must, you die,
    That day an innocent shall be killed.
BILL JENKS: Unless today's the day, there's bigger fish
    To get the griddle under. Bankruptcy
    For one.
SIMON:          It's coming sooner than you think.
BILL JENKS: What's coming sooner? Bankruptcy? Or death?
SIMON: You get no more prognosticating, Jenks.
    Now, do your worst. I'm all strapped in.
    *In whose name do you cast out spirits, Healer?*
BILL JENKS: What do you mean? The usual. JC
SIMON: LIAR!
BILL JENKS:    I don't name names. I've got the gift.
    I cast out demons in my own damn name.
    —Is that what you wanted to hear? Stand back.
    I've got the gift. It's mine from my conception.
    The powers picked me out, and since the womb
    I stand above humanity and spit.
    I cast out demons in my own damn name.
SIMON: I FLEE!
BILL JENKS:    Don't flee! Don't *flee*! Nobody said to flee!
    Come on! Have you got a message for me?
    Prophesy! Gimme a tip on the market!
SIMON: JAN? JAN? DARLIN'?
BILL JENKS:                    Wait a minute, wait—
SIMON: Where's Jan?

BILL JENKS: Excuse me, I was talking to—

JAN *enters;* DOC *and* STACY *close behind.*

SIMON: Jan? I'm cold. I'm—

JAN: Simon? Simon?

SIMON: I FLEE.

BILL JENKS: NO!

JAN: SIMON!

SIMON: JAN? I LOVE YOU—

BILL JENKS: Demon!
Come back!

SIMON: Back where?

BILL JENKS: Not yet!

JAN: Simon!

DOC: *Simon?*

BILL JENKS: I'm talking to the goddamn demon, Jack!
—Just a general sense of—up or down?
Buy or sell? Telephones or hot dogs?

SIMON: Jan, I'm tired. I'm thirsty. I love you, Jan.

JAN: I'm here. Simon?

SIMON: Jan. I'm cold. I'm *cold.*

BILL JENKS: I got a conversation going here!

STACY: Doctor? Is it Simon?

DOC: Yes, it's Simon.

BILL JENKS: Just—back *off*—

DOC: It always has *been* Simon—
But this is Simon after a miracle.

STACY: But cool, but neat, but so *je ne sais quoi!*

SIMON: Stacy? Jan—? Jan—

JAN: Simon . . . Simon . . .

BILL JENKS: Everybody: Take a minute here—

JAN: Simon, have you been *cold* . . . *all* this time?

BILL JENKS: DEMON, DEMON, GIMME SOMETHING
      HOT!

BLACKOUT

# PART III

## SCENE 1

*Another year later.*

*Split scene: Left, peepshow talk booth (*BJ*'s hallucination) in* BILL JENKS*'s living room. Right, front porch of* BJ*'s rural home outside Dallas.*

*Lights up stage left:*

BILL JENKS *loads quarters into a slot as a screen rises on a peepshow talk booth, revealing* MASHA *in a silk robe and platform shoes.*

*Each holds a phone receiver.*

BILL JENKS: Slut . . . slut . . . slut . . . slut . . . slut.

MASHA: You realize, of course, you're nothing but a faggot,
    The balled-up, writhing, Adolf Hitler kind.

BILL JENKS: People eat you in their fantasy.

MASHA: You're sloppy drunk.

BILL JENKS:                     I'm paying for the call.
    . . . You want to hear your story?

MASHA:                     All I hear
    Is your brain sizzling like a T-bone.

BILL JENKS:                     Listen, child:
    I'll tell you the repeating saga of Masha.

MASHA: Preacher's comin', duck and cover, boys.

BILL JENKS: You like to blame us for yourself, then run away.
You're always breaking free, breaking out,
I'll show you the pattern. First, you busted free
From Daddy; then a hot-rod boyfriend, maybe,
And then one of your teachers, and then some artist
Who painted you nude, then some criminal
Made his living jackin' Coke machines,
Then Sylvester of the Purple Prairie—
Then you ditch your pimp and come to me,
So you can break my chains and fly away
Into the cage of your latest master and captor.

MASHA: What about your pattern, honey?
Jack 'em up like monkeys till they're jumpin'
High as Heaven on that down-home Bible jive—
Cleanse me save me change me fix me, preacher,
Use me, preacher, eat my wallet, suck
My sorry sap.

BILL JENKS: 　　　　You slinky slut.

MASHA: Unbind 'em, heal 'em, fleece 'em, and forget 'em.
All God's chillun got a pattern, sugar.
All God's chillun got to walk a chalk line.

BILL JENKS: Slut slut slut slut slut!
—I'm sorry I'm sorry I'm sorry I'm sorry I'm sorry!
I deeply regret the misunderstanding that led to . . .
The misunderstanding.

MASHA: How long do we have to stay tangled together?

BILL JENKS: Until I fathom what the knot is knit of.

MASHA: Look . . . I got tired of *preaching* in my ears,
The mindless mechanical bark, bark, bark.
OK? Don't make it into a work of art.

Don't make me a testimony to the lie
You're living.

BILL JENKS:       Lie? What lie, you Jezebel?

MASHA: Everybody's selling a fantasy.
Your trouble comes from hating the glistening
     guts
Of that one gospel fact. You'll happily
Confess to dealing crap to your disciples,
But you won't witness to the simple truth
They're selling it all right back to you,
They're the closest thing to God you've got—
The audience is everyone and no one—
Anonymous mother you're suckled by and hate
And love. You want to see a whore? Go seek
Among the pews. They sell themselves to you.

BILL JENKS: Crawling on your belly like a Jezebel.

MASHA: At least I don't fall down to a phony God.
You bow to them. You fear their punishment.
You take the blame because they see a lie
While looking in your direction.
It ain't your lie. It's just their fantasy.
*You* want to go to Hell because *they're* stupid.

BILL JENKS: Masha, Masha, what has become of you?

MASHA: I was a part of your pattern—thanks for the save.
Thanks for the exorcism and the gray suit.

BILL JENKS: Heck, you ain't halfway exorcised. I'd give
An estimate of twenty-five percent,
If that. Hell, you're a carnival of demons.

MASHA: It's Satan's world. You buck the tide you get
All waterlogged and wrinkled up. And drowned.

BILL JENKS: You ride the flow and paradoxically
       You end up burning in a lake of fire.

MASHA: Tell me you've lived one day in fear of Hell.

BILL JENKS: I sure have lived in fear. Mostly in fear
       Of Heaven and its possibilities
       For boredom and monotony and Sunday
       Every day, and Jesus hanging around.
       . . . I can just about smell you through the glass.

MASHA: What are you talking about?

BILL JENKS:                           Is it bulletproof glass?

MASHA: Do you have a gun?

BILL JENKS:                    A lot of people do.
       How's the security here? Do they protect you?

MASHA: Who? Where? Why on earth would I need protection?

BILL JENKS: Who? The demons who employ you here.
       Every sex emporium needs security.

MASHA: What are you talking about, what are you *on*?
       I DON'T WORK IN A SEX EMPORIUM.

*Lights down on* MASHA. BJ *alone in his living room with a*
*phone in one hand, bottle in the other.*

MASHA'S VOICE: I've got a house, and I've got a minivan
       And twenty-three pairs of shoes. I'm legally married.
       I am the wife of the executioner
       For all of Texas, and I am the president
       Of the Texas Citizens for Victims' Rights.
       All you see of me is your fantasy.
       That's all any of you ever see.
       I should rob banks!—nobody ever sees me.
       I'm like one of those Rorschach ink-blot messes
       Showing the twisted story in your head.

## ALL YOU'RE SEEING IS THE STORY IN YOUR HEAD!

BILL JENKS *hangs up and crawls toward the door with his bottle.*

BLACKOUT

*Lights up stage right:*

BILL JENKS*'s front porch, next minute:*

*Off and on throughout scene,* JOHN *works on his cross (it rests against the rail), attaching tokens to it with contractor's glue. His hair grown shoulder-length, and sporting a beard, he still wears his prison whites.*

JOHN [*sings*]: *If I got paid a nickel*
　　*Every time you told a lie,*
　　*I'd put those nickels in a sack*
　　*And tie that sack around my neck*
　　*And jump into the river*
　　*And sink beneath the water,*
　　*If I got paid a nickel*
　　*Every time you told a lie.*
　　*If I got paid a dollar*
　　*Every time you made me cry,*
　　*I'd pile those dollars in a stack*
　　*And climb that stack and grab the moon*
　　*And hide the moon in Houston*
　　*Where you could never find it,*
　　*If I got paid a dollar*
　　*Every time you made me cry,*
　　*If I got paid a nickel*
　　*Every time you told a lie.*

*Meanwhile,* BILL JENKS *crawls out of the house and across the porch, lugging his bottle, and sits bracing himself against a post.*

BILL JENKS: Woman claims to be the proud possessor

Of forty-six shoes . . .

JOHN [*sings*]: *I'd put those nickels in a sack*

*And tie that sack around my neck*

*And dive into the ocean*

*And mingle with the fishes*

*And tell 'em all my troubles*

*'Bout a woman who deceived me*

*Every time she told a lie.*

BILL JENKS: . . . Who's come for a little BJ?

Come get a little BJ!

Come on and get a quality BJ!

Where are my innumerable followers

To take me back in a tearful ceremony?

I got a zillion bucks, and I can't touch it.

My attorneys won't return my calls.

I held a press conference. Who was there?

Who was there, John?—wasn't it a guy

From the *Neo-Nazi Tribune*, something like that?

*The Sword and the Blade. The Cross and the Ball,*
shoot,

*I* don't know. *You* get the sense of it.

JOHN: Would you shut up?

BILL JENKS:                  I might. It all depends.

JOHN: The suckers love you, Bill, so just shut up.

We'll always love you. That's what makes us suckers.

BILL JENKS: If I got paid a nickel

Every time you kissed a pickle . . .

If I don't pull somebody outa their grave,
I might as well get in it, too.
JOHN: You've gotta train your mind on Huntsville, Bill.
In twenty days they strap my mother down.
If you're gonna raise somebody from the dead,
It might as well be my mother, right?
BILL JENKS:                              Look here.
What was your mother in for, in the first place?
JOHN: You know what she was in for.
BILL JENKS:                         No. I don't.
Her current fame obscures her former fame.
JOHN: It wasn't nothing she was famous for.
Vehicular homicide. To be exact
You'd say vehicular infanticide.
BILL JENKS: Vehicular *infanticide*? O, God,
Sometimes can't you feel the English tongue
Kind of licking around inside your stomach?
JOHN: Is that enough to say?
BILL JENKS:                   Well . . . What'd she do?
JOHN: Ran over my baby sister with the Chevy.
Pretty much on purpose. So she drew
A twenty-five-year slide. She almost made it.
But then they charged her with another murder,
They claimed she killed that empty-minded girl—
That nameless, brainless Jane Doe, may the Lord
Have mercy—claimed my mother perpetrated rape
And murder with a broomstick. That is false.
Even over a couple dozen years
And twenty prison walls, her innocence
Travels out to me like radiation.

BILL JENKS: Bathes us in its sacrificial light.

JOHN: Laying in the dirt, drunk and sarcastic.

BJ *aims around with a Derringer, miming shots.*

BILL JENKS: Bull's-eye. Bull's-eye. Bull's-eye.

      I just have one more thing to say about Masha:
      She used to say "mushmeller" for *marshmallow*
      And her name was Mar-sha, not Masha.
      And she had thighs like marshmallows, which
      I never touched one time, not even dreaming.
      Announcement!—I have never read the Bible.

JOHN: Is that thing loaded?

BILL JENKS:              Always assume it's loaded.

JOHN: Well, then, unload it please. [*BANG*] Thank you, you hick.
      . . . The way of a fool is right in his own eyes.

BILL JENKS: Proverbs, chillun.

JOHN:                   Proverbs, 12:15.

BILL JENKS: The proverbial Proverbs.
     [*Lies back*]
                  Hey—Ow! Watch the head!
     Man, that's black. That sky is solid velvet.

JOHN *examines* BJ—*passed out—takes the gun, considers attaching it to the cross. He points it at the dark. BANG.*

HT'S VOICE: STOP. DON'T SHOOT.

JOHN: Who's out there? Come up here and get killed.

*A space of silence.*

HT [*sings*]: *Wake up this morning*
     *Blue dog called my name*
     *If you ever get to Houston*
     *Boy you better walk right*
     *You better not gamble*

[*He materializes from the dark.*]

. . . You better never have no fun a-tall.

. . . Wrap yourself around me! Gimme a squeeze!

I waited for you at the Huntsville Greyhound!

Man, I broke parole to see you. Man—

Baby baby baby—how you doing?

I'm doing good, myself! I'm traveling!

They call me Hostage Taker 'cause I took

Some hostages, and that's my claim to fame.

Who is this guy? How come he don't talk?

Brer Jenks has got hisself a Tar Baby.

[*Sings*] *Mistah Blue-bird on mah shoul-dah!*

OK OK OK let's settle down.

I waited for you! First the Houston bus

And then the Dallas, and you never came!

That's the day things started going wrong.

Parole boss say be here, or I'll get mad.

You miss the meeting and he gets his sharpened

Fingers motorvating on that phone pad

Wop bop-a-lu-bop, a wop bam boom!—like *that*

He violates your ass, and you got warrants.

That's what happens when the bus don't come!

—How long has Brer Jenks been like this?

JOHN: I saw you on TV.

HT:                                    —Now, don't believe

Just every single thing that TV shows you.

JOHN: I didn't say believe. I say I saw.

I saw you on there.

HT [*with* BJ's *jug*]:         Want a snort? . . . To fame!

Woo. Woo. That strangles up your vocal cords.

JOHN: How'd you get here, anyhow?

HT:                                        I walked.

   I walked across the fields. Across, across.

   That's why I'm all red dirt up past my knees.

   . . . They let you wear your hair and beard in the joint?

JOHN: No. I been out a couple years.

HT:                                        A couple?

JOHN: Yeah. Two years.

HT:                             Then what you wearing whites for?

   Been gambling? Gambling treats you mean as drinking.

   Either one, your wardrobe goes to hell.

   Now, look at me. I'm mussed, I know, but look—

   A brand-new suit. Use me as your example.

   [*Siren in the distance.*]

   —That's that blue dog calling me. That skinny

   Blue dog . . . [*Of the cross:*] It's kinda Mexican, ain't it?

JOHN: Yeah, it's Mexican. And so's my mother.

HT: So's my mother? What'd you say about—

JOHN: No, *mine*. *My* mother's Mexican, not yours.

HT: How do you know my mom ain't Mexican?

   She could be an African-Mexican.

   I could be an Afro-Hispanic-American,

   So leave each other's mother out of it.

   Did you just see a worm crawl outa my brain?

   Some days I feel screwier'n Japanese jazz!

   Been starin' in the pit of Hell so long

   My eyes are bleeding and I'm damn near blind,

   But that's all right . . .

   Let me introduce myself.

JOHN: You introduced yourself.

HT: I introduced myself? OK, OK,
     Then let *you* introduce *yourself* to *me*.
JOHN: I'm John Cassandra.
HT:                                    And this here's Preacher Jenks.
     Me and the preacher have a history.
     I'm charmed I'm sure. 'Cause I heard all about you,
     Uh-huh, the Cross Boy and the preacher man.
JOHN: What's your purpose here?
HT: My purpose on this earth?
JOHN:                          No. On this porch.
HT: I'm just here long enough to cure my nerves.
BILL JENKS: My age, you get to feel this vernal weather
     Down in the gristle . . .
HT:                          Brother Bill!
BILL JENKS:                              Quite so!
     Is it autumn, or is it spring? I can't decide.
     We've got this barometric memory
     That kind of senses atmospheric change
     Based on what we've seen since childhood.
JOHN:                                         Bill,
     Will you shut up?
HT:                     How long has he been like this?
BILL JENKS: It's a proper question.
JOHN:                        No, the question
     Is how long are you gonna *stay* like this?
BILL JENKS: Either until autumn or until spring.
     Old HT! I saw you on the TV.
     Let's us have a drink.
HT:                     Brer Jenks! I'm out!
     . . . You're out! We're out! It's time! —We hit that number!

Baby, don't you remember? I finally hit that number.
I pulled some mischief, slick as baby shit—
Guess where? Do you know where? In Canada!
Been up there for a year. I got a car,
I got a name, I got ID, the total package,
I had it all up there, but I missed home.
Not home in Willard. Home back at the Walls.
I missed that smell. The voices echoing.
The same day over and over and no way out.
I kind of missed that feeling like you're trapped.

BILL JENKS: What I hear, you ain't gonna miss it long.

HT: I feel like I'm full of poison—emotional poison,
Physical poison, and every kind of poison.
My mind got fat. My dick won't make no juice.
What are they *thinking* about in Canada?
They make you feel ridiculous . . .

BILL JENKS: It wasn't Canada that made you famous.
There ain't no show called *Canada's Most Wanted*.
Nope, I believe they showed your photograph
On one they call *America's Most Wanted*,
Had it on now several Sairdy's running,
Account of this thing you did in Ellersburg,
And not the Canadian Ellersburg, no sir,
This other Ellersburg down here in Texas,
The Texas Ellersburg. A quite bad thing.

HT: *I* know. —Well, it looks like . . . well, it looks like . . .

BILL JENKS: *Well*, HT, it looks like a double killing.
It looks like they think you did it, like they think
You did this double killing up there. So they think.

*Siren in the distance—*

HT: It was a desperate situation, Brother Jenks.

BILL JENKS: They're looking for you, Brother Hostage Taker.

HT: Don't go believing everything you hear.

JOHN: Sirens? Sirens are hard not to believe.

HT: That's just a train. The good old K.C. Flyer.

BILL JENKS: They want you, they want you bad, the worst. "The
      most."

HT: I'm saying it was a desperate *situation*.

BILL JENKS: How could it be desperate? There's nothing *there*,
    It's *Ellersburg*—a crossroads with a store,
    A gasoline pump, and a Coke machine.
    It's like a scene from 1957.
    Thing still dispenses Yoo-Hoo for a dime.

HT: Man, you don't get it, I'm *here*, I'm *here*.

BILL JENKS: And Mom and Pop slopped over on the floor—
    Which one was Mom? Which one was Pop? We'll wait
    On Ellersburg's most talented mortician
    To figure that one out.

HT:                 He had a gun!

BILL JENKS: Hey, so do I. You gonna blow my head off?

HT: What are you saying? Man, we have a deal!
    Twelve months in a prison cell together—

BILL JENKS: Hey now, what was that movie, what was that
      movie . . .
    *The Defiant Ones*, with Sidney Poitier.
    "Charlie Potato, Charlie Potato!" . . . Boys,
    I'm going to Huntsville, Texas, boys,
    To raise this bastard's mother from the dead.

JOHN: Thank God!

BILL JENKS: No. Get back. There's foodstuff caught in your
     beard.

JOHN: Thank God. Thank God!

HT: So—where do I come in?

BILL JENKS: Come in?

HT: Come in. Come in.

BILL JENKS: You don't come in.

HT: I don't?

BILL JENKS: You don't come in. Where would you fit?

HT: That's what I'm asking in this stupid place
     With sirens screaming awful bloody murder
     And blah blah blah—now where do I fit in?

BILL JENKS: Sidney . . . You've got no role in my movie.
     My movie's got a cast of one.
     It's all about this preacher silhouetted
     Against a gory sunset outside Dallas
     Tyin' up a rope to lynch himself.
     That's the picture I'm trying to get across.
     Kind of a tragic silly mystery.

HT: Man, we have a deal, we have a deal!

BILL JENKS: What deal? When did I ever make a bargain
     With such as you?

HT: Man!—twelve months in a cell?
     A solid year? Me smelling your shit
     And listening to you playing with yourself,
     Coughing, farting, talking in your dreams,
     Crying all night long the first eight weeks?
     —And I remember the night you didn't cry,

First night you slept the night entirely through.

I didn't sleep all night that night, for joy.

BILL JENKS: Ah! Those were the days! And then they stopped.

HT: Brother, Brother. I waited at the Greyhound . . .

Do you want to know why those people got killed?

BILL JENKS: There was this guy I knew, he was a—well, *you* know,

I don't know what you'd call him, maybe a faggot?

That what you are? A homosexual?

HT: O, God, O, God, this ain't my people here!

I got to get with my people, not these people!

Gimme a *sign*!

. . . Do you know why that mom and pop got killed?

Can you ever guess why those two persons died?

BILL JENKS: 'Cause buckshot blew their brains up.

HT:                                                        Can you guess?

Or should I trace it back for you? Listen:

I'm all set up, I got a job, I'm in a suit,

I'm in the Houston Public Library.

Carpet. Silence. Air-conditioning.

Holding *Street Rod News* in my black fingers.

The time has come to buy a powerful new

Machine, because I'm free . . . White guy comes over.

Now, I'm just looking at my magazine—

I'm looking at pictures of engines, powerful engines—

Look up, 'cause now he's going hem-hem-hem

With his throat. I say to myself: White man

Coming up in the public library . . .

Light brown hair, blue eyes, the one

Explain your options on the life insurance,
Sell you a washer-dryer combination.
I'm thinking, First my beautiful suit, and now
This white man in the public library.
Not young, but not exactly middle-age,
Just nonchalant, you know, ain't nothing to him.
He says, "This is my name," and all like that,
White man in the public library.
"Don't get me wrong, I gotta show you something.
Come over here to this part of the library
For compact discs and videos and all,"
And I don't know is he a *cop*, some *Mormon* . . .
What am I gonna do but follow him there?
He leads me like we're on safari, man,
We're gonna capture something with our stealth,
White man in the public library.
Like we're stalking on a quiet field of birds
Or moving through a church,
And there, across the room,
White man in the public library
Shows me a beautiful young black woman.
She's standing by the racks, what can I say,
Looking like a lump of Lawd Have Mercy.
Short sleeveless dress of graphite gray,
Smooth black arms, incredible black face,
Had that sticky-outy posture like she tore
Herself from *Vogue* or *Ebony* or *Cosmo*;
The tiniest littlest dab of spit would melt her.
He showed her to me.
He looks at me with this face,

Like a bird dog saying with his face, There,
Master, I didn't leave
No marks of my teeth in her feathers.

JOHN:                                    . . . Then what? . . .
        What then?

HT: Then we stood still. And then she moved. And then
        She passed into the rest of things.
        And him, he's gone like he weren't never there,
        White man in the public library,
        And I felt very confused. I said, I said,
        "I *can*-not stop being confused by this.
        I stand here in my slick new suit, so clean . . .
        A white man shows me a black, beautiful woman . . ."

JOHN: The same suit you have on.

HT:                                    This very suit.

JOHN: There's not much left of it.

HT:                                    Why, no, not much.
        It's done been eat to bits in all the confusion,
        The ongoing saga of my continuing
        Confusion, which has not stopped, from then till now,
        You see, because I continue to feel confused.
        They'll never let me out, I don't suppose.

BILL JENKS: Nope. Calendars and clocks, my man.
        And bars and walls and years, et cetera.

HT: Do you understand a little better now?
        Now do you understand why I killed those people?

JOHN: I know who understands: God understands.

HT: God is just a little jumped-up white man.
        That was God in the Houston library.
        White man in the public library.

. . . I can't stop the thoughts,
I'm cookin' too hot!
[*Leaving*]
*My* suit? . . . Take a look at yours!

BILL JENKS: Give you a sign? Here's a sign . . . He gone—
Into the sea of Spam and Wonder bread . . .
Sidney. Sidney. I ain't Tony Curtis.
I'm strictly Looney Tunes! I'm Daffy Duck!
Woo-woo! Woo-woo.

*Sirens; train whistle.*

JOHN:                        . . . Give me something of yours.

BILL JENKS: Something? My what. My shoe? What something?
    What?

JOHN: Something that's lucky or important or that means
    Something.

BILL JENKS:        Lucky.

JOHN:                    Like your Derringer.

BILL JENKS: I'm not sure I'm in favor of gun control.

JOHN: We glue it to the cross, and you'll be healed.

BILL JENKS: I'm not sure I'm in favor of being healed.

JOHN: This is how the Mexicans cure their troubles.

BILL JENKS: By gluing items on the cross. With Jesus.

JOHN: Trinkets, yeah, things that have touched them, tokens,
    Things to represent their scars and glories.
    To sacrifice. To crucify their sorrows.

*Train whistle.*

BILL JENKS: . . . It's always the most relentlessly simple things
    That tear at you and break your heart. Like trains.
    [*Sirens*]
    SO LONG, SIDNEY!

JOHN:          Maybe he can't be helped.
     But did you really have to be a shit?
JOHN *exits into the house.*
BILL JENKS: . . . Where on earth did you get that silly notion?
     Don't you know what the emblems are about?
     They don't stick pagan symbols on the cross.
     Them Catholics have the whole thing codified,
     Everything's got a meaning—all this stuff:
     These crossbones are the bones of Adam,
     Said to be buried at the foot of the true cross.
     These are the hammers and these the nails that banged
     The Savior to the tree in agony.
     These aren't lucky dice—except for the guy
     Who won his garments—they cast lots, remember?
     The Roman soldiers gambled for his clothes.
     They stripped Christ bare, and one went home a winner.
     Where do you get this stuff? Here is the sun
     Whose face the storm obscured when Christ was killed,
     And here is the moon that bled. Where do you get
     Your silly notions, John? . . . The moon that bled.
BILL JENKS *raises his Derringer, takes aim: CLICK.*


BLACKOUT

# SCENE 2

*Twenty days later.*

   *Corner of Tenth and J Streets in front of Walls Unit,
Huntsville, Texas.*

   JOHN CASSANDRA, *costumed as a clown, poses on his cross.*

*Hubbub, voices* O.S. *[fading out]:* Shoot her full of poison,
   Throw her in a grave!
   Shoot her full of poison,
   Throw her in a grave!
   [*others:*] Two! Four! Six! Eight!
   There's no rhyme or reason
   To capital punishment!
   Two! Four! Six! Eight!
   There's no rhyme or reason
   To capital punishment!
   [*others:*] Justice for the innocent!
   Killing for the killers!
   Justice for the innocent!
   Killing for the killers!
*Lights up on Public Information Office across the street
from the Walls:*
   JERRY *and* STEVIE. JERRY *at the window.*
JERRY: Stevie, has Texas gone and joined the circus?

Or is it the universe, or just my life
That's grown a populace of runts and freaks?

STEVIE: Jerry, should I toss this coffee out?

JERRY: I have a daughter, Stevie: you touch my daughter,
I'm gonna jump straight up somebody's ass.
Is that a concept of too wide a girth
To fit inside our brains?

STEVIE:                               Well, I don't know.

JERRY: You *kill* someone, someone kills *you*. Come on.
Has justice run away and joined the circus?

STEVIE: I couldn't say. I don't know. Maybe so.

JERRY: Do you call life in prison "punishment"?

STEVIE: I'd never actually touch your daughter, Jerry.

JERRY: You'd better kill 'em: Send 'em all to Hell,
If Hell awaits them, and be done with it.
. . . Here come the preacher man. O, looky here.
I'd like to thump this guy. If I was bigger,
Man, I'd grab his legs and bounce him on
His head until his children's crying stopped me.
Good afternoon, good— Huh-uh, man. No way
I let you in with liquor on your breath.

BILL JENKS [*having entered*]: *You* have liquor on your breath, I
think.

JERRY: A lunchtime margarita don't equate
To waltzing in here zigzag stinkin', partner.
You'd like a little coffee.

STEVIE:                               I tossed the coffee.

JERRY: She tossed the coffee. Bubble us up some more.

STEVIE: Maybe for later, you mean?— Right now it's almost—

JERRY: —Haven't got the time. The hour is nigh.

You've made the acquaintance of the son?—I think
The word I'm looking for is "colorful."
You'll pale beside him, pardner. Alley-oop.
This way. We're at our maximum
Or we'd have half Ukiah, California,
Squooching their butts down in the seats. *Ukiah.*
That'd be Indian for "cracker." Maybe "Okie."
My people generate from Tennessee,
Just like Elvis Presley and Davy Crockett.

BILL JENKS: Elvis generates from Mississippi.

JERRY: Elvis came from Memphis, Tennessee.

BILL JENKS: He was born in Tupelo, Mississippi.

JERRY: Jesus Christ was born in Israel,
But that don't mean he ain't American.

STEVIE: I'm not sure we have the time for this.

JERRY: Stevie, how long is the woman going to be dead?
. . . Go on and round 'em up. We'll be along.
[STEVIE *exits.*]
—Enough. Will you at least concede that Elvis
Presley was a *son* of Tennessee?

BILL JENKS: I so concede.

JERRY:                          All right, enough dispute,
All right—my daughter gave me this, no sense
Offending her bounty. Silver-plated. Cheers!
Go on, raise you a toast to Mississippi.

BILL JENKS: Mostly I've lived my life in California.

JERRY [*as they move*]: O, well, I've never been to California.
Right this way—look down, these sonabitchin'
Paparazzi will fill your eyes with moons—

I mean, I might get out there, maybe for
A ball game on the order of the Series
Or a playoff, if Texas could field a decent team,
But all we have is the Rangers and the Astros.
[*They enter the Witness Room, joining* JOHN *(still*
*costumed as a clown) and* STEVIE.]
What are you supposed to be? A clown?

JOHN: We're here to raise my mother from the dead.

JERRY: *Ukiah*, that'd be Indian for "Him
Who Picks His Nose and Eats It."

JOHN:                                         Who's this guy?

JERRY: The PIO.

STEVIE:          A son, here: this is John.

JOHN: The PIO?

STEVIE:          You know the Reverend.

JOHN: The PIO?

JERRY:          I think we need this man
Struck from the list.

JOHN:                         The pee-eye-eeh-eye-oh?

STEVIE: The Texas Department of Criminal Justice's
public information officer.

JERRY [*to* JOHN]: You're the one who parked his big old
cross
Down there out front. I'm gonna have it towed.

JERRY *has pushed a buzzer. The curtain opens on the death*
*chamber.*

   BESS CASSANDRA *lies tied down on the gurney, the head*
*of which cranks up to make her visible;* WILL BLAINE *in*
*attendance.*

BESS: Who put me here? I didn't do anything!

Jesus God! I didn't do anything!

WHY DO I HAVE TO DIE? WHAT DID I DO?

JERRY: Will—now, haven't we got her tranked?

WILL:                                                     She's tranked.

BESS: They said I'd die, and then come back to life.

BILL JENKS: Who told you that? Who told you, Ms. Cassandra?

BESS: I don't know. I heard it in a dream.

I don't know who was talking in that dream.

BILL JENKS: I'm Reverend—

BESS:                                         Shit. I have no need of Jesus.

I'm paying for my own goddamn sins.

BILL JENKS: Ms. Cassandra? May I call you Bess?

BESS: Sure, please do. Who else is in the room?

JOHN: Hi, Mom—Hi, Mom—remember me?

BESS:                                                               O, sure.

You kind of look familiar. Is that John?

JOHN: Hi, Mom.

BESS:                     You got real big.

JOHN:                                         I know.

Mom, we're here to raise you from the dead.

JERRY: Cut the mic, please . . . Fellas, listen up:

Reverend, how did you get on the list?

This woman doesn't know you.

JOHN:                                             She's my mom,

And he's the family's spiritual counselor.

JERRY: Across that chamber in the other room

I've got the Reuters, UPI, AP, the Huntsville

*Courier*; down in that baking street

I've got the TV news and video from France
And Germany and every goddamn place,
And I'm not gonna have an incident
For these assholes to be reporting. Clear?
. . . Go on now, give us back the audio.

BESS: Hello? Hello? That was a little scary.
. . . John, are you the only of my children
To make the trip?

JOHN: I guess I am.

BESS: OK.
I wasn't expecting trumpets and a crowd.

JOHN: I think they harbor some resentment due
To certain things that ruined their childhood, Mom.

BESS: John, I always thought you were retarded.

JOHN: I'm not retarded. I just had big teeth.
They made me talk real slow. But now I'm grown—
Grown up—and so . . .

BESS: You've grown into your teeth.
. . . Where'd the Reverend Preacher go?

JOHN: He's praying in the corner, Ma. We've come
To raise you up when they pronounce you dead,
Because we know you didn't hurt Jane Doe.
We know you're innocent.

BESS: I'm not so sure.
I know I'm guilty of vehicular
Infanticide, because I do remember
Squashing little Amy with the car.
. . . Amy. What do you think she'd look like now?

JOHN: Amy? Amy would resemble rotten bones.

JERRY: Folks, we're looking at just a couple minutes.

BESS: You children bothered me, I don't know why.
        I'd start off every morning with the notes
        Of music in my heart, and I was young,
        But minute by minute my mind would get all red,
        And photographs in magazines would make me cry,
        Until my life was squeezing all my blood—
        Now, isn't that peculiar, don't you think?
        And here the little children all around.
        I should have killed you all while you were sleeping.
        I guess I didn't really think things through.
        I don't know why I thought I had to use
        The car. Do you believe in demons? Well,
        Nothing in this world can take away
        The deeds I've done. They don't belong to demons.
        I won't give my crimes to Satan.
        I'm keeping my crimes for me.

JERRY: It's six p.m.

STEVIE:            May God have mercy on you.

JERRY: I'll just read the order of execution.

BILL JENKS: The order? Isn't that the warden's function?

JERRY: The warden's water-skiing off Honduras.
        Or else he's scuba diving off Belize.
        Vacationing, in other words. It falls to me
        To read the order of execution. Stevie,
        Will you please read the order of execution?

STEVIE: Isabel Cassandra, formerly
        Residing in Odessa, Texas:
        Having been convicted of the charge
        Of murder perpetrated in the course

Of aggravated sexual assault
Upon Jane Doe (name and address unknown),
Be informed that the Sovereign State of Texas
Undertakes to execute the sentence
Imposed July 19, 2001; to wit:
That you shall be confined until this day,
Maintained in health, granted communication
With family, legal counsel, and the press,
And then, upon this day, at such an hour
As suits the warden, you shall be called forth
And taken to a place prepared for such
Administrations as shall have the swift
Result of death to you; and therein put to death.

JERRY: May God have mercy on you, Bess Cassandra.

WILL *lowers the head of the gurney;* BESS *lies prone.*

JOHN: Mom, are you prepared?

BESS:                              What part of me
Can be prepared? I can't talk to this part
Or that part, I can't say, "Get ready, arms
And legs, get ready, guts and lungs and liver—"
Can't even cross my hands over my chest.
. . . Well, thanks for coming by to say goodbye.

JOHN: Woman, if I could say goodbye to you
I would've said it thirty years ago.

JERRY [*low, to* BJ]: The sodium thiopental's going in.

BESS: John?

JOHN:        Mom, Mom . . .

BESS:                              Why are you dressed like a clown?

JOHN: There's reasons for it, Mom.

JERRY:                              She doesn't hear.

JOHN: It's something I've got going.

STEVIE:                              She can't hear you.

JERRY [*low, to* BJ]: Next pancurium bromide will collapse
        The lungs and diaphragm. And finally
        Potassium chloride stops the heart.

BILL JENKS:                              How long?

JERRY: Seven minutes from the start to finish.

JOHN: . . . Seems like seven minutes are almost up.

BESS: . . . Am I supposed to be dead? When do I die?
        . . . I still don't think I'm dead. I think—O, hey,
        My I-V thing popped out. It did. It's out.
        Your poison's spilt all over.

WILL'S VOICE:                              I-V team!
        Get your unit reestablished, please.
        Never mind. Stand down. I'll reconnect.

BESS: Will it hurt—uh—will it hurt the mattress?

*The curtain closes across the window.*

BILL JENKS: Mr. PIO. What's going on?

JERRY: Will? We gonna have to clear the site?

WILL'S VOICE: Negative. Sixty seconds.

JERRY: All right. Stevie—go and see about the boys.
        Who's over there?—it's Blake for UPI,
        I think, and *damn* it, *damn* it all to Hell—

STEVIE: I'll see if we can't close the lid.

JERRY:                              O, yeah.
        Another perfect termination. Thanks.
        I owe you, Steve.

STEVIE:                  You do. You'll pay me, too,
        Tonight at Mursky's.

JERRY:                  Drinks are all on me.

STEVIE *exits.*

JOHN: Hello? Hello? What's going on in there?

JERRY: This thing's been a fiasco from the start.

JOHN: Why can't the guy at least say hi or something?

JERRY: I've never seen the like, and I was here
     For Karla Faye. A healer and a clown.

BESS'S VOICE: Uh-oh. O NO.

JOHN:                              Mom? Mom? —What's going on?

JERRY: I can't stand to hear you squawking
     About it in my ears no more!

JOHN: You don't act like a government official!
     You act like a baby!

JERRY:                    *I* act like a baby?
     TORCH THE JAILS AND LET'S BE DONE WITH
          IT!

JOHN: There's something funny going on in there!
     Did you just hear the mic switch off? HELLO!
     [*Bangs on the glass*]
     HELLO HELLO GODDAMNIT HEY HEY HEY—

*The curtains part abruptly to reveal* HT *with an arm locked
around* WILL BLAINE's *neck and a long, crude stiletto shoved up
under* WILL's *chin.*

HT: I AM THE NIGGER OF DEATH!
     [*To* WILL] . . . Let's let the public get a look at you!
     You hiding back there like the Wizard of Oz.
     [*Sings*] *Let the Midnight Special*
     *Shine a light on you*
     *Let the Midnight Special*
     *Shine his ever-lovin' light on you.*
     Welcome! Welcome! Welcome to my show!

BESS: I hope you know this wasn't my idea.

JOHN: You're still alive!

BESS:                          And really loving it.

BILL JENKS: Hello, HT. What are you playing at?

HT: A little game that I'm inventing called
        Let's Execute the Executioner.
        If anybody interrupts the game
        I'll blow up every motherfucker here
        Including me.

JOHN:                  You're gonna blow us up
        With a knife?

HT:                  I didn't say I blow you up
        With a knife. I blow you *up*, is all I said.

JOHN: Well, what's that in your hand?

HT:                                  Don't get sarcastic.

JOHN: Hey, I'm not. I'm quite sincerely trying
        To form some sense of what you're threatening
        To blow us up with here today, and what
        I'm seeing in your hand looks like a knife.

HT: Quite true. But what's this in my other hand?
        [*He releases his choke hold on* WILL *and pulls a gun from*
           *his pocket, points it at* JERRY *while keeping the point*
           *of his knife to* WILL*'s chin.*]
        I want everybody in this room with me.

JERRY: We can't do that.

HT:                  You can't when you're dead!

JERRY: We can't, sir, it's impossible. The chambers
        Don't communicate.

HT:                  What are we doing *now*?

JERRY: There's just no access. They're designed that way
    With just this kind of contingency in mind.
HT: How about this contingency!
HT *shoots. The glass doesn't break.*
JERRY:                          That one, too.
HT: But I still got this guy! His head ain't bulletproof!
JERRY: Of course. We're all cooperating here.
HT *fires all his bullets uselessly at the glass.*
HT: You think I'm outa bullets? Well, I am!
    But whatchoo think these honeys are? Big tits?
*Having dropped both knife and gun, he finds in his pockets two
hand grenades.*

*He yanks the pin of each with his teeth and spits the pins at*
WILL.
    Nothin' clamps these levers down but me.
    Anything happens to me—I get distracted,
    Maybe you bore me and I fall asleep,
    Sharpshooter shoots my *head* off—we *all* die.
    Now get around in here. Yes—you and you.
    [*To* JOHN] No—you, sir—no. Don't want no clowns in here.
    The Reverend Mister Billy Jenks. That's right.
    Go out that door, go down the hall, and come—
    You think I'm stupid? No. I'm just insane.
    Go out that door, and come around in here!
    You don't say boo to *no*body. Or else!
JERRY: You have my word.
HT:                          I have your what what what?
JERRY: Stay calm. We'll do as you request.
    You have my word as a Texan.

HT:                              O . . . OK . . .

JERRY: OK, Preach, let's get on under the Big Top.

JERRY *and* BJ *exit.*

HT: . . . Ma'am, I'm sorry to mess your execution up.

BESS: O, that's OK, I guess.

HT:                              Well, I'm just saying.
      I'm just improvising, so I hope
      You don't resent some wrinkles in the plan.

BESS: I'm not in a position to resent much of anything.

HT: Hey, if you want, I'll make these folks untie
      Your arms and legs and kiss your ass.

BESS:                              No, thanks—
      All in all, I'd rather be put to sleep
      Than blown to bits.

HT:                         Yeah . . . Ain't you the lady
      Flushed her little baby down the toilet?

BESS: No, that wasn't me.

HT:                         You put it in
      The trash incinerator.

BESS:                         Guess again.

HT: The grinder in the sink.

BESS:                         Not even close.

HT: Where *are* those guys?

WILL:                         It doesn't really matter.
      I'll have you on the gurney soon enough.

HT: The gurney? For probation violation?

WILL: I saw you on *America's Most Wanted.*

HT: Is there no person on this earth who ever
      Watches any other program? Try
      And hide! I'm like the president!

WILL: You're guilty of a double homicide.

      Today should be your execution day.

HT: The day's not over yet.

WILL:                You goddamn right.

HT: You make my point. You see these things?

      I splay my fingers, on the count of five

      We mount to glory on a hand grenade.

WILL: That's fine with me!

JOHN:              Hold on, hold on!

WILL: I'll get blown up as long as you do, too.

HT: I think we're in agreement here. Let's die!

BJ *and* JERRY *enter.*

HT: Don't move, don't anybody move! I swear to God!

      . . . Hey, hey, Reverend Billy Jenks, did you

      Imagine the trajectories would bang

      Us face-to-face on execution day?

BILL JENKS: You get me believing in things like fate, HT.

HT: I know. It's just too marvelous for words,

      The crowning thing that sets it all aflame!

      Actually, I heard it on the news

      How you'd be here and all, that's why I came.

BILL JENKS: Will Blaine.

WILL:             Excuse me, Preacher, I've got business.

HT [*to* WILL]: O no you don't! You don't go back in there!

      You do not press that button. No you don't!

      Not as long as you live! Right here. Right here!

      Did I see your hand mashing on that button?

JOHN: Mom? Are you all right?

BESS:              Who? Me?

JOHN: Talk to me. Don't just lay there.

BESS:                                    Blah blah blah.
     How's the weather? Blah blah blah your health.
     How are they treating my Johnnie at the circus?

JOHN: When men go murdering murderers, they mock
     God's saving work and make a clown of Christ.
     That's the message. That's the statement.

BESS:                                       Well,
     I'm glad I lived to hear the explanation.

JERRY: What are your demands?

HT:                          Uh-huh . . . Demands?

JERRY: Have we surprised you with the question?

HT:                                          Yes,
     I'd have to say you kind of did.
     [*Monitor sounds a flat reading: beeeeeeeee.*]
     You pressed the goddamn button, didn't you?

JOHN: Why'd you press it, fool?

WILL:                        It's what I do!

JOHN: . . . NO! . . . Don't cover up my mother's face!

JERRY: This woman is deceased.

JOHN:                          But—seven minutes!
     Seven minutes! You said seven minutes!

JERRY: In general the process takes that long—
     But often Phase One stops the heart, and then—

HT: And then they screw you out of five or six!
     They gyp you! . . . Bring this woman back—
     Dose her up with speed or something! [*To* WILL] You!

JOHN: That's exactly what we came here for.
     . . . Hostage Taker, this is the very thing
     That brought us here. The Reverend Jenks is powered
     To deal with demons and restore the sick,

I've seen him do it with a word, a breath,
Two years I've dogged his steps, I've watched him work—
Deafness, stammering, cancer, withered limbs—
I've seen him pinch their one last mustard seed
Of faith and scatter it into blossoms—
Blindness, palsy, lunatic torments—
And I believe this man can raise the dead.

BILL JENKS: With your permission—

HT:                                     Do it to it.

WILL: She's dead. This ain't a coma.

JERRY:                              LET HIM TRY.
. . . Leave it alone, Will. Let this run its course
And you and me go get a drink at Mursky's.
Country-western, and scotch in plastic cups.

WILL: I'm sick of cowboy music.

JERRY:                          Let him try.
. . . We've done a bunch of these.

WILL:                          A couple hundred,
Right around two hundred.

JERRY:                          Let him try.

BILL JENKS: No—leave the shroud.

HT:                          . . . Go on. Go on.

BILL JENKS: . . . One time, when Jesus healed, he said, "Who
        touched
My garment? Something just went out of me—"
He stood in a crowd pressing from all sides
But knew a particular touch had drawn his power,
Sensed a healing had gone out from him . . .
All I have is a knack for crossing paths
With people just about to heal themselves.

A gift for sticking in my head and smiling
Just when someone's gonna snap the picture.
I've never healed one person of one thing
In all my lying life.
If I had, I'd feel it, wouldn't I?
Wouldn't it jump a little in my blood?

WILL: This gets me in my guts. Get up from there.

JERRY: Two hundred? Is it really as many as that?
You ever walk the rows at Joe Byrd Hill?
How many rows have we ourselves laid out?
I bet you'd hike a half a mile of graves
Fed by our work, Will Blaine, yours and mine,
And then you'd come to a couple of plywood boards
Hiding the hungry place that waits for this one.

BILL JENKS: . . . Lord, it's all about that open mouth.
We don't want to die and go in there.
They claw down with a green-and-yellow John Deere
Backhoe and scoop a darkness under the grass,
Takes six or seven seconds to produce
The only thing on earth that lasts forever.
God in Heaven, we beg you to widen your eyes.
Look here at this woman put to death
By bureaucrats. See her. Remember her.
You made this woman's life—remember that.
Make her now, again. GOD, GIVE HER BREATH.

HT [speaks in BESS's voice]: . . . Don't raise me up! I want to stay
in Hell!

JOHN: No! She's not in Hell!

HT/BESS:                            I always was.
I lived my life in Hell. But now it's simpler.

WILL: You're channeling through the black guy, Mom.

JOHN: There's no such thing as channeling. That's Satan
    Talking in my mother's voice.

BESS:                              It always was.

JOHN: It's just a trick of demons.

WILL:                    We have demons?
    We don't have mediums, but we do have demons?

JOHN: I just take it as it comes.

WILL:                You do?
    From where? You take it as it comes from where?

JOHN: From Genesis and Exodus. No channeling.
    No mediums. No ha'nts. No clanky chains.
    Men and women; devils; angels; God.

HT/BESS: Hell is full of music. Lonely music.
    Hell is full of sadness. Full of truth,
    Full of clarity. Hell is beautiful.

BILL JENKS: I know this son of a bitch. It's *you*.

HT/DEMON: [*facing* BJ]: *C'est moi*! The one who really loves
    you!—

BILL JENKS: The blue dog of Huntsville.

HT/DEMON:                  The demon of Simon's
    coma.

BILL JENKS: The demon of money.

HT/DEMON:              The demon of your fame.

BILL JENKS: You've run me all my silly goddamn life—
    *Why*?

HT/DEMON: I really can't quite say; it's just
    There's something about your style that pisses me off.

BILL JENKS: All my silly life.

HT/DEMON:           And now no more.

I'm all through pimping you, Jenks—you're on your
own!

JOHN *cries out, flings himself against the glass. All freeze.*

HT/DEMON: Now my work of half a century
Culminates. Warden, blow the whistle!
Beloved William Jennings Bryan Jenks:
You've come to failure, and today you die.
Beloved, my most interesting project,
My signature, my sunny revelation:
Count your heartbeats. Today you die.
Your breath stops. Your sight blackens, then burns
With visions since your birth, and you'll be met
At every turning with the leering truth:
Not one prayer you've uttered ever prized
The slimmest chink in you, not one escaped
The maze. They suffocated in their coffins.
The start to finish of your life's design
Tributes nothingness. And now the dark.

HT *opens his fingers. Grenades fall.*

BILL JENKS: Liar! Liar!—I never raised the dead.

BESS *sits upright and the shroud falls away.*

BESS: AMY? . . . Where'd she go? She was right here—

*Silence. Blinding light.*

BLACKOUT

# EPILOGUE

*Corner of Tenth and J, later that night.*
    STEVIE *stands behind a microphone,* JOHN*'s cross nearby.*
*Light from video crews, flashbulbs.*

STEVIE: Can't we get this monstrosity out of here?
    People are tripping over it left and right.
    This is blasphemy. This thing's a scandal.
    [VOICES *ad lib* . . . ]
    Quiet! —I'm sorry. —Goddamn you! —I'm sorry.
    Here is the information we've got for you.
    This evening, shortly after five p.m., an as-yet-
        unidentified prisoner overcame and stabbed to death a
        guard in the Walls Unit, who remains nameless until
        notification of family. Thereafter this prisoner gained
        access to the execution chamber in this corner of the
        unit, right behind me, and . . .
    You have the statement. You have the statement . . .
    [VOICES *ad lib* . . . ]
    Now, Mrs. Blaine has asked to say a word, wife of
        William Blaine, who supervised our Teams in the unit
        there— She's the wife of Will Blaine, a very special
        employee of, a very . . .
    The wife of Will Blaine, the widow, the wife, the

widow . . . President of the Texas Citizens for Victims'
Rights, Marsha Hollings Blaine.

MASHA *comes up, well dressed, with well-coiffed, abundant hair.*

VOICES *ad lib . . .*

MASHA: I say today an innocent has been killed!

Today is a Day of Judgment on us all!

[VOICES *ad lib . . .*]

Look at you all!—like wasps on watermelon!

[VOICES *ad lib . . .*]

Rahr! Rahr! Rahr!—like *curs* on *carrion.*

I LOST MY HUSBAND IN THAT PLACE TODAY.

. . . Maybe he's in a better place. Who knows?

. . . Some people go around with this idea

The Milky Way is just some big machine,

And we're being eaten alive by this machine,

Trodden down and gutted out and gobbled

And scattered out along beside the road

To fertilize the ditch, and that's our fate:

And I say, God above, let it be so!

Let there be no Resurrection Day!

[VOICES *ad lib . . .*]

LET THERE BE NO RESURRECTION DAY!

If Bill Jenks thinks that he can raise the dead—

Let him raise himself! WE'RE WAITING, BILL.

Let him raise *someone*, and then I'd say

That he was onto something—wouldn't you?

[*Of the cross*] Look here, look where someone's set up
   the means

Of execution in the gory Bible days.

Here they hung them after they'd been scourged.

You know what scourging was? They whipped the skin
Until it ripped, and then they whipped the muscles
Underneath, until their whips licked bone.
And then they hammered what was left up here,
And broke the legs of what was left, so that,
Without support, it slowly suffocated.
And that's the boy the power of whose blood
You plead, an executed criminal . . .
[VOICES *ad lib* . . . ]
LET MY HUSBAND ROT IN THE GROUND UNTIL
    HE'S MUSH,
Let him rot in the ground till he's gravy,
Until he clarifies like honey in the heat
And dribbles into dirt that doesn't feel
A thing or think a thought.
May the dirt I called my husband never wake,
May that dirt stay dead until the whole
Universe collapses into cinders,
May the weight of general emptiness
Strive and grind against itself and work
The cinders down to black, stupefied darkness,
May he be dead until the final thought of God,
As long as his assassins stay dead, too.
. . . When Texas trips the lever of the blade,
And that blade dives down through a killer's neck,
And that neck pumps that evil blood six feet,
And that head goes rollin' into the world,
What drives that blood is the beautiful heart of Texas,
And staring out of that head are the eyes of Texas.
The dead face of the killer we have killed—

This is the face of liberty and justice.

This is the beautiful face of liberty and justice!

*Weeping, she makes a smile and strikes a pose.*

BLACKOUT

- END -

# PURVIS

*Purvis* was developed by Campo Santo, the resident theater company for San Francisco's Intersection for the Arts (executive director Deborah Cullinan; founders Margo Hall, Luís Saguar, Sean San José, Michael Torres), and premiered at Intersection in February 2006, with the following cast:

| | |
|---|---|
| Cully Fredrickson | Lyndon Johnson; Ohio State Patrolman |
| Catherine Castellanos | J. Edgar Hoover |
| Michael Shipley | Clyde Tolson; Pretty Boy Floyd |
| Daryl Luzopone | Melvin Purvis |
| Danny Wolohan | John Dillinger |
| Michael Torres | Job Interviewer |
| Vanessa Cota | Blanche; Captured Woman |
| Delia MacDougall | Baby Face Nelson |

Collaborative Team: Nancy Benjamin (vocal director), Michael G. Cano (stage director), Jim Cave (lighting design), Valera Coble (costume design), James Faerron (set design), Jeff Fohl (video/photography), Dan Hamaguchi (graphic design), David Molina (sound design), Jennifer Orr (properties design).

Production Team: Nora Hailey (assistant stage manager), Vanessa Cota, Melyssa Jo Kelly, Courtney Luna, Lorrie Jean Marinas (production team), Kevin Heverin (research advisor), John Ingle (violin music), Adam Palafox (research).

Directed by Delia MacDougall

Melvin Purvis (1903–1960) began as a special agent in the U.S. Justice Department. In 1932, J. Edgar Hoover placed him in charge of the Chicago office of Hoover's new Division of Investigation, which soon became the FBI.

Over a six-month period in 1934, Purvis's pursuit of the nation's most famous "Public Enemies" put him in the national spotlight. Apparently envious, Hoover drove him from the bureau the following year.

After leaving law enforcement, Purvis married and raised three children, making his living as a radio broadcaster and as the head of the "Junior G-man" public relations campaign for Post Toasties cereal.

Some important dates:

**June 1933**—Under the suspected direction of Charles "Pretty Boy" Floyd, gangsters ambush police and agents transferring a prisoner in Kansas City, killing three policemen and Special Agent Ray Caffrey, the first "G-man" to die in action.

**March 1934**—The bank robber John Dillinger escapes from jail in Indiana and crosses a state line, making himself a federal fugitive.

**May 1934**—Under Purvis's direction, federal agents ambush Dillinger and Lester Gillis—aka "Baby Face Nelson"—at the Little

Bohemia Inn on Little Star Lake, Wisconsin. Both criminals escape while two bystanders are killed. Later that night in a second gunfight Nelson kills one of Purvis's agents before escaping again.

**July 1934**—Purvis heads a team of agents and local police who assassinate John Dillinger outside the Biograph Theater in Chicago.

**October 1934**—Purvis participates in the killing of Pretty Boy Floyd in a cornfield near Wellsville, Ohio.

**November 1934**—Baby Face Nelson dies in a shootout with federal agents on an Illinois roadside. Two agents also die.

**February 29, 1960**—Purvis dies of a bullet wound from a .45 he received as a gift from fellow agents when he resigned. The death is ruled a suicide, though some evidence suggests it may have been an accident.

In seven scenes, *Purvis* follows history backward from 1966 (six years after Purvis's death) to the evening of the "Bohemia Inn Shootout" in 1934.

# CHARACTERS

Lyndon Johnson
J. Edgar Hoover
Clyde Tolson
John Dillinger
Melvin Purvis
Job Interviewer
Pretty Boy Floyd
Ohio State Highway Patrolman
Baby Face Nelson

A lynched black man
An office secretary
A woman bound and gagged

*Scene 1: October 1966*
*The White House Oval Office*

*Scene 2: March 1, 1960*
*The home of J. Edgar Hoover*

*Scene 3: February 29, 1960*
*A fathomless void*

*Scene 4: Spring 1959*
*An office at KSBC radio, Florence, South Carolina*

*Scene 5: January 1935*
*An office of the U.S. Division of Investigation, Chicago*

*Scene 6: October 22, 1934*
*A cornfield near Wellsville, Ohio*

*Scene 7: May 1934*
*A hotel suite on Little Star Lake, Wisconsin*


*An ellipsis [ . . . ] beginning a line is meant to suggest a pause.*

You may break your heart; but men will go on as before.

—Marcus Aurelius

# SCENE 1

*October 1966: The White House Oval Office.*

   *In a small zone of light,* LYNDON JOHNSON *and* J. EDGAR
HOOVER *play gin rummy,* HOOVER *in a business suit,* JOHNSON *in
shirt and necktie, socks, undershorts.*

   JOHNSON *pours himself generous drinks of bourbon.*

HOOVER *sips sherry.*

   *A lynched black man hangs in the dimness just outside the
zone illuminated.*


JOHNSON: The Mormon angels landed here from Mars.
    They claim to bring a major revelation,
    But look you close: It's just so old it's new.
    Naturally they revive polygamy.
    They're polishing up the ancient creeds
    And revving up the old dictates,
    Virgin sacrifice and every scary
    Type of genital mutilation and
    Putting your hand on your balls when you swear a lie.
HOOVER: —Elvis Presley is a clever robot.
JOHNSON:                         Mark me,
    The aliens wouldn't touch the Eastern Bloc:
    They ain't nuts, just incomprehensible.
    They've never said so much as boo to *us*.

They've got to have some outfit fronting them.
Who sends his ticklish tendrils in behind
The phony fronts? Our man J. Edgar Hoover.
I want the goddamn Mormons infiltrated.

HOOVER: Lyndon, do you mean to indicate
The Church of Jesus Christ of Latter Day
Saints has extraterrestrial origins?

JOHNSON: I mean of course I don't mean Mars *per se*.
Just outer space. And if they're emissaries,
Then they've got outer-space angelic leaders,
Someone who dispatched them here from blackness.
Soon's they're ready, they'll negotiate,
And I mean to say negotiate with *us*.
We'll find the outer-space administrators
And cut ourselves a deal. We'll dangle them
The Soviet Union and one thousand virgins.

HOOVER: You overestimate our populace's
Moral amplitude.

JOHNSON:                    One *hundred* virgins.

HOOVER: And you anticipate the politics
Of creatures we can't even guess about.

JOHNSON: Nope. They're good old boys in search of profit.
If they were commies they'da lost the space race.
I don't care how many arms and feet
And slimy orifices God supplied you,
It's hope of raw materials and markets
That drives the steam from out your rocket's asshole.
Gin.

HOOVER:  No thanks.

JOHNSON:                    That's gin for me.

HOOVER:                                    Make mine

  Another sherry . . . No. This isn't rummy!

JOHNSON: Three fours, four jacks, a run of spades.

HOOVER:                                         Go fish!

JOHNSON: Now why, when fortune blows a little stink

  Up your kimona, do you seek to change the game?

  Falling behind should goad your appetites:

  Sting you to whap the shit off the butt of your jeans

  And hook that bull by his nostril ring.

HOOVER:                                    You brew

  One nauseating mess of metaphors.

  . . . We've got bigger fish to fry than Mormons.

JOHNSON: Martians.

HOOVER:              Lyndon, Mr. President,

  You spoke of leaders. Let us *speak* of leaders.

JOHNSON: A hunnerd twenty-five and—flip them—three,

  And thirty—hunnerd fifty-eight for me.

HOOVER: I'll not disperse among the Mormon fold

  A hatch of undercover Martian-hunters.

  They'll end up married to a bunch of milkmaids.

JOHNSON: We've got Andromedans athwart our women.

  They breed with Mormon females to make monsters.

  Stick your spyglass in amongst that mess.

HOOVER: My fondest vision is to map the hairs

  And very capillaries of the least

  Significant citizen and begin a file.

  To tongue and probe the grossness in the soul

  Of every enemy of the American Dream.

JOHNSON: And what exactly is the American Dream?

HOOVER: I've just described it.

JOHNSON:                          Tonguing, probing—

HOOVER: Infinitesimal infiltration

And alphabetization of the masses.

But not the Mormons—yet. Someday; my word.

Now, Lyndon. Mr. President.

JOHNSON:                          That's gin.

HOOVER: Gin?

JOHNSON:        I play the hand that's dealt me.

HOOVER:                          Dealt?

I dealt you gin, a pat hand, one two three?

JOHNSON: The odds come long, but once upon a time

We all were zygotes in a long-odds race.

People may complain, J. Ed, but think:

We're each the luckiest sperm there ever was.

HOOVER: You S.O.B. You stacked the goshdarn deck.

JOHNSON: How did I stack a deck I never held?

HOOVER: Thus we hear your enemies crying.

JOHNSON:                          Stud.

—A hand of stud. All right, you're high: Queen bets.

HOOVER: Queen, sir?

JOHNSON:        I'm sorry, *King* of Spades. Your bet.

HOOVER: Mr. President, I wouldn't bet

A hamster's giblets on the King of Spades.

JOHNSON: . . . Don't you think I know what brings you here?

I've dealt with darkness ever' step along.

Every ounce I've laid on the side of clean

I've goddamn nearly had to match with dirty.

The Civil Rights Act, 1964:

There the scale bangs down decisively

For victorious good. My life is right.

—I'm paired.

HOOVER:                    It's lowball, and the pot is mine.

*Phone rings.*

JOHNSON: You love to monkey with the rules . . . [*On phone*]
    What say?

    . . . I see. And don't we have our whole Sixth Fleet

    Playing war games down along those parts?

    . . . No. I won't. Keep me apprised. That's all. [*Hangs up.*]

    . . . My legacy is civil rights for all.

HOOVER: Martin Luther King has got to go.

*Phone rings.*

JOHNSON [*on the phone*]: Who's this? (Go on and shuffle please,
    J. Ed.)

    Yes, Admiral, I am aware. The submarines,

    The nuclear. I'm rattling our saber.

    —This is your president. Alert the fleet.

    Mao has got to know the ocean's ours.

    [*Hangs up.*]

    We all agree you've got me where you want me:

    How do you like my starburst undershorts?

    I don't bawl, I'll take my punishment

    For letting a weasel get me by the eggs.

    But I can have a dab of shellfish compound

    Here in my palm by two this afternoon

    (Thanks to the chemists at the CIA)

    To make it look like heart conditions killed me;

    And I won't even have to lick it up:

    It sinks into the flesh. And sink it will,

And I sink too, before I let the weasel

Devour my entire house. My deal.

HOOVER: Those vicious chemists at the CIA.

JOHNSON: Chairman Mao can kiss my bony ass.

—I'm on a little junket Saturday.

Georgia, Tennessee, the Carolinas.

HOOVER: Just the time of year!

JOHNSON:                    The votes down there

Just might stay Democrat another decade,

Although we smell a sea change.

HOOVER:                    Lovely weather.

JOHNSON: Smooch the infants, snip the ribbons, suchlike.

Dedicate this one museum there. This feller

Elvis Purvis is the hero of it.

Down around where he called home. The man

Who collared Dillinger. Remember him?

HOOVER: Several agents collared Dillinger

With the assistance of the whole division.

Later Purvis murdered Pretty Boy Floyd.

I have the officer's written recollection,

The Kansas cop, or whatever state it was.

On Purvis's orders, he dispatched the wounded

Prisoner with a bullet to the brain.

JOHNSON: A perjured recollection?

HOOVER:                    Written. Signed.

And decades later, Purvis shot himself.

I take that as the plainest mea culpa.

JOHNSON: The South Carolina Criminal Justice Hall

Of Fame. The Elvis Purvis Gun Display!

—Elvis? That his name?

HOOVER:                              His name was Melvin.

JOHNSON: I'll be saying words in praise of him.

   The nation sighs; let's celebrate our heroes.

   Purvis; Kennedy; Martin Luther King.

HOOVER: We want straight arrows, Boy Scouts, true believers.

   What we can't abide are vivid heroes.

   If a man should stand too high, well then,

   We'll lop him at the legs. As I did Purvis.

JOHNSON: A preacher ain't nothing to fret you, Herr Director.

   Preachers rise and fall.

HOOVER:                              King's dangerous.

JOHNSON: They sit themselves on golden toilets, wiping

   Their holes with hunnerds, talking on two phones

   While flying around in bright red jet airplanes,

   Don't pay no tax on half a cent of it,

   Nobody says boo. What shoots 'em down?

   What finally shoots 'em down? It's good old poon,

   The whores and mistresses and altar boys.

   You'd like to hound and tree a man already

   Besieged by willing females who'll destroy him,

   These underfucked and overfed and half-

   Way unzipped Baptist slatterns shyly come

   To sprawl themselves upon his offices.

   And some of 'em are sexy. Comely. Cuddly.

   Here you want to take him in your crosshairs

   And thunder him to earth, with all

   The messy implications that implies.

HOOVER: The population is a nightmare seething

   On the earth. We can't let heroes rise to wake

   The monster into chaos.

JOHNSON:                    "I have a dream . . ."

HOOVER: Man's best ordered into hives and warrens.

    Public schools, vast corporate factories,

    Housing projects . . . concentration camps . . .

    I'm going to knock with three.

JOHNSON:                         Let's see, let's see,

    That's twenty points. You'll catch me soon.

HOOVER:                                    I'm bored.

JOHNSON: I come from westward-roaming pioneers.

    I like to sling my big old Eldorado

    Around the roads on my place, hollering

    And firing my revolver and raising dust

    And gunsmoke. You won't get me in a hive.

HOOVER: I'm not going to infiltrate the Mormons.

JOHNSON: The last assassination crippled us.

    [*He lifts the receiver and dials.*]

    [*On phone*] What news? . . . Is that a fact? Well, well.

      I swan.

    He must be facing some internal strife,

    Some rumbling among his favored generals.

    Try the following: Sweep the guns of the fleet

    Across their bows. If they keep coming, raise

    The subs and let them see our nukes. [*Hangs up.*]

    . . . So freedom is a dusty artifact.

HOOVER: You'll have your Civil Rights Bill, Excellency.

    You just won't have your heroes. You must suffer

    The lack of such as King and Kennedy.

JOHNSON: I miss John Kennedy. I miss his wife.

    They think I rigged his killing. They'd believe that of me.

HOOVER: And yet you've done much worse.

JOHNSON: The other thing.

HOOVER: The other thing. The undiscussable matter.

*Phone rings.*

JOHNSON: The Martians aren't our only misery.

    [*On phone*] . . . Let him come. What say we weigh his
        pecker?

    . . . Turn them subs toward the mainland now
    And prime the missiles. Let him see our eyeballs.
    [*Hangs up.*]

HOOVER: Friend, let's discuss the undiscussable.

JOHNSON: I wish I *had* killed John F. Kennedy.

    And Lincoln. And Caesar. Murder in pursuit
    Of power, well—

HOOVER: It's easy to imagine.

JOHNSON: That's why they imagine it of me.

    The other thing is past imagining.

HOOVER: The other thing is undiscussable.

JOHNSON: Speaking of artifacts and speaking of peckers,

    What's the story on Dillinger's remains?

HOOVER: Ach! Purvis is responsible for that legend.

    He let reporters photograph the corpse.

JOHNSON: May we all have such a legend told of us.

HOOVER: He made it necessary that each daily tour

    Of FBI headquarters should begin
    With a denial of that vulgar fantasy.

JOHNSON: You mean it's merely a *tale* that Dillinger . . .

HOOVER: That he was marvelous between his legs?

    That his gigantic organ was collected,

And in a jar in some museum we have set
Adrift his pickled genitalia?
. . . No, my president, the tale is false.

JOHNSON: I understand the Great American Novel
Is *Moby-Dick*.

HOOVER:           I disagree.

*Phone rings.*

JOHNSON [*on phone*]:       What news?
. . . Not yet. I smell a bluff. Just stay the course.
[*Hangs up.*]
Mao Tse-tung will get Taiwan. He'll swallow
Vietnam and a chunk of southern Russia,
But Mao will by God never get my balls—
[*Phone rings.*]
[*On phone*] —you hear? . . . I won't give in. Let's stare
him down.
[*Hangs up.*]
Them goddamn sonabitching commie Chinks.

HOOVER: Sir, the greatest error of our century
Was Truman's failure to bombard the horde
In 1953.

JOHNSON:    You mean with nukes.

HOOVER: I do. MacArthur would have finished them.
Instead, from that seed of mercy will grow all
The terrors of the third millennium.

JOHNSON: Right in here's the famous crimson button.

HOOVER: Aren't there wires?

JOHNSON:              No. It's wireless.

HOOVER: Aren't you going to let me see?

JOHNSON:                              They change
     The combination daily.
HOOVER:                    Well, I'm sure
     That I could get it for you.
JOHNSON:                    Sir, I *have* it.
     I'm the president.
HOOVER:            Quite so.
JOHNSON:                    I'm just
     Not certain where they put it.
HOOVER:                         But it's here.
JOHNSON: Of course it's here. It's *for* the *president*.
HOOVER: I've put it in the major newspapers.
     The *Times*, the *Post*, the London *Times*. And *Pravda*.
JOHNSON: Well, that's insane. But harmless. Can't set off
     A war with a combination. Got to have
     This button that the combination's *to*.
HOOVER: I mean the other thing. I've sold you off.
     I have discussed the undiscussable.
     I've given it all to the press. Tomorrow's headlines
     Will stretch six inches tall to tell the world that—
JOHNSON: Never mention it anywhere nor ever.
HOOVER: I think a headline in the *Times* and *Post*
     Will constitute a mention, will it not?
JOHNSON: . . . And *Pravda*, too?
HOOVER:                    Just to amuse myself.
JOHNSON: Manure! Why would the organ grinder
     Grind up his monkey in his organ?
HOOVER:                         Maybe
     The monkey made too many metaphors.

JOHNSON: Folks say the Gila monster never shits,

> So everything inside him turns to poison.

HOOVER: There you go again.

JOHNSON:                             You've done it? Really?

> You're sick enough, I grant you.

HOOVER:                            God, you'll never know.

JOHNSON: I do believe you've gone and done it. I . . .

> I'll be slaughtered like a roach. The mobs
>
> Will mutilate the relics of my flesh
>
> In hope of hurting every molecule.

HOOVER: What you did would merit exactly that.

JOHNSON: I'm bottled up. You've left me skinny choices.

> [*Phone rings. Rings. Rings.*]
>
> I'm going to murder myself in the Oval Office.
>
> I'm going to murder you, too.

HOOVER:                         With a telephone?

JOHNSON: You and everybody else. [*On phone*] Who now?

> —Well howdy hi. Yes, General, I'm sure
>
> You know I've spoken to the admiral.
>
> . . . Then don't ask questions either of us could answer.
>
> Ask me something you don't know, for instance
>
> When to conference call me with the other
>
> Lily-livered commie-loving Chiefs
>
> Of Staff. Let's say at eight-oh-five p.m.
>
> —If I can start and finish Armageddon
>
> By eight-oh-five, then you can orchestrate
>
> A conference call by then, by God. Hop to!
>
> [*Hangs up.*]
>
> You've brought down Armageddon on my head.
>
> Might as well have jabbed the big red button.

HOOVER: Is it actually red?

JOHNSON:                      I've never seen it.

     —Why don't we take it out for a little spin?

     [*Phone rings.*]

     [*On phone*] We need a fifth of Jack and a jug of sherry.

     . . . All right then. Prime our Third Configuration.

     . . . I shit you not. The firstest puff of smoke

     You spy from out their smallest little popgun

     I intend to answer with a nightmare. [*Hangs up.*]

HOOVER: Third Configuration? Isn't that—

JOHNSON: Let's us do what Truman orto've done.

HOOVER: Won't that spark a Soviet reprisal?

JOHNSON: Spark a reprisal? Sir, at the end of this finger

     I've got thirty-two thousand, one hunnerd and ninety-three

     Sonofabitchin' nuclear warheads, and

     Them Russkies pack about two thousand more.

     Betwixt us we've heaped up some twenty-four

     Thousand megatons of nasty business.

     That's twenty-four million Hiroshimas in

     This little box, under a little button.

     That kind of megatonnage leaves no Northern

     Hemisphere. Spark a reprisal? Sir,

     I'll spark a God-consuming conflagration.

     I'm going to murder everyone in the world.

JOHNSON *gulps from a flask.*

HOOVER: Shellfish compound?

JOHNSON:                 No, sir. Mineral oil:

     The recipe of crow and shit you fellers

     Fustigate my stomach with requires it.

     It'll grease your stuffing and send it along.

[*Phone rings.*]

[*On phone*] . . . Yes. I'll use the red phone. [*On red
    phone*] Señor Khrushchev!

Herr Khrushchev! —What's he— Translator?—

(Well, he's unloading just a bit of thunder.)

This is between me and Mao. Here's a little

Formula to follow, Comrade Khrushchev:

Restraint equals reward. Now, Translator,

Make him understand he's come between

Mao and me, and he should sit this out.

. . . If that's the attitude he cares to strike,

God help the Northern Hemisphere. [*Other phone
    rings.*] Hang on.

[*A receiver in either hand*]

It's eight-oh-what? . . . Well, I'm impressed . . . Hi,
    fellers.

"Joint Chiefs of Staff." I hear that phrase

I can't prevent my mind from picturing

Pygmies with a spear . . . Indeed I have.

We're chatting now . . . The red one, yes indeed.

What color's yours? . . . (They're remonstrating with me.

. . . I'm not going to run for a second term.

I dislike this office. I want corners.

I don't like a goddamn oval office.)

[*A third phone rings.*] Revelation Central; Jesus speaking.

—Hey! "Huberty Humphrey sat on a wall,

Huberty Humphrey had a great"— Howdy, Hue.

[*He's now dealing with three phones—a receiver in each
    hand and one laid on the desk before his face.*]

[*On phones*] That wart-face Russkie hasn't got the sand.

We backed him off on Cuba. Here's the thing:
I don't give one dab of rat shit whether
We kiss our grandkids in their beds tonight
Or burn the ocean, earth, and sky to cinders.
[*Throws phones aside.*]
Sir, are you a Christian man? Make peace
With your creator. Where's the combination?

HOOVER: I've come all over shaking.

JOHNSON:                                    Here we are.
They change it every goddamn day.

HOOVER:                                    I'm all
Aquiver and atingle and aglow!

JOHNSON: This is the selfsame finger I itch my ass with.

HOOVER: And that's the magic button!

JOHNSON:                                    THERE SHE LAYS.

HOOVER: Push it with your member! Rape it! Rape it!

JOHNSON: Mao may get Taiwan—but he'll never get this!

HOOVER: My!—there's megatonnage *there*, good sir!

JOHNSON: I'm gonna drive this thing to Hot Goddamn!

HOOVER: I'm all afire, and abashed. I'm all aswarm,
I'm prancing in a madness! Shall we dance?
A jittlejot of junko juice
A snittlesnot of turn-me-loose
A razzledazz of hello mom
And there you have your atom bomb

JOHNSON: I've just destroyed the Northern Hemisphere.

HOOVER: The world is ending, and I'm in your arms.
[*Music plays. They dance together.*]
. . . I've a confession, darling. April Fools'.
I didn't hand your secret to the world.

JOHNSON: It's October.

HOOVER:               I'm a kinky boy!

JOHNSON: You didn't tell the *Post*? No *Pravda*?

HOOVER: I was only joshing. Now you've gone
      And diddled with the button! —Are you cross?

JOHNSON: . . . What does it matter? Sooner or later
     . One of us was going to flush the toilet.

HOOVER: Round and round and down the spout—hurrah!

*They dance near the phones;* JOHNSON *grabs one.*

JOHNSON: How goes our business? . . . What? He's turned
      around?
      Turned around? But what about our nukes?
      . . . All right, rescind the order . . . Well, goddamn.
      Then don't rescind it, if it wasn't sent.
      . . . What do you mean? Indeed I gave the order.
      [*Hangs up.*]
      Apparently this thing's not functioning.

HOOVER: Which thing exactly now?

JOHNSON:                 Ha-ha. Ha-ha.
      Somebody's got a load of explaining to do!

HOOVER: You've got a little explaining to do as well.

JOHNSON: Johnson broke the button with his Johnson.
      . . . Have we amused you? Good. Go home. Go on.
      . . . Get on out, J. Edgar. I must nap.

HOOVER: . . . If the commies get us, it won't be by war.
      They'll get us in the brain, right in our soft
      Impressionable minds. They'll get us in
      The coffeehouses and the beatnik poems.
      Our spoiled little hairy little children

Dancing in the psychedelic light.
A fond adieu, Your Excellency.

HOOVER *exits.*

JOHNSON: I don't feel so excellent today.

[*As he dons his clothes, he addresses the hanging corpse.*]
. . . Hook the jug by the ear and hoist it up
For a little smooch. Wonder what I'd do
If somebody ordinarily decent ever
Entered here? Feller like that Purvis.
'Pologize for entertaining in
My skivvies. Turn my liquor breath away.
President of travesties and favors.
Faithful of the balance. Figuring it
To tip down finally on the attractive end.
Unreasonable, childish hope:
And bless you, sojer, may you never spy
The thumbs of bought historians and hostage
Propagandists weighting the boonful side.
I'm traveling to the South week after next.
O, I'll meet Purvis marching in the sunshine:
Son of light, master of undisguise . . .
The South, well—down there, certain airs bring back
The sweetness of a childhood I no longer
Find at all believable, of years
I must have dreamt. —Why did I ever waken?
O, I was a knobby little man.
Sir: I put the skinny in skinny-dipping.
Flailing in my slow descent, screaming,
Splashing, the cooling shadow of the bluff

Blanketing us and it all echoing . . .
I used to like to be the last to leave.
I'd stay there lonely with my chin on my knees,
There by that slow water at the bend
Where right about that time of afternoon
The dragonflies dipped down to drink.
And I'd come running for my father's house,
Hot all over again in the last light,
Thudding like a quarter horse for home,
Falling flat and slurping up the crick.
Lord, that water went down sweet.
. . . Never since then a truly slakable thirst . . .

JOHNSON *fades from view, leaving visible only the hanging corpse.*


BLACKOUT

# SCENE 2

*March 1, 1960: The home of* J. EDGAR HOOVER.
   HOOVER *in silk kimono and garish face paint.*

HOOVER: THE CLOWN IS DEAD!
TOLSON [*entering*]:          Jay?
HOOVER:                Shot himself!
*Phone rings offstage.*
TOLSON [*exiting*]:               I'll get it.
*In the course of the scene,* HOOVER *cleans his features and changes into a business suit, preparing for the day's appointments.*
   *His housemate* CLYDE TOLSON *attends.*
HOOVER: Marvin the clown has blown his own clown head off!
   Clyde, ring up the *Post*. Ring up *The New York Times*.
   I want those rats to promise me he stays
   Entombed on the obituary page,
   Or certainly never crawls as far as four,
   That he rises no higher than five, not one page higher,
   And keeps to the lower half. One column inch.
   No photograph! —The clown without a face.
   I want this cloaked and shrunken in the stench
   Of his self-murder. *And*: no Dillinger!

Dillinger broke the law, the law broke him:
Let the glory be the law's, and not
Its instrument's, the late, lamented Marvin.
I own he was a modest instrument.
He didn't slaver after glory, merely
Postured himself so it accrued to him.
—Do you know what the poor wretch was reduced to?
Tomorrow his admirers will read
That after a stint with breakfast cereal
He wandered into radio. Somewhere
Down south he kept the farmers in the know
And jazzed it up for barnyard animals.
O, my God, the leader of a horde
Of Junior G-men! Lovely! —Suicide!
The Baptists promise Hell for that, I think.
Dear God, I pray he was your Baptist son.
"Onward Junior G-he-he me-hen
Marching as to war! With the cross of Pur-vis—"
Purvis was the perfect name for him.
He was perverse: He purposely, perversely
Projected a lovelorn, stoic decency;
I believe it to have been primarily prideful,
Perverse and prideful. Are you calling the *Post*?
No mention of museums! —The the the the
South Carolina—nothing of the kind.
"On then, Junior G-men, on to victory."

TOLSON [*reentering*]: Jay—Jay—Jay—Jay . . . Melvin Purvis has
    died.

HOOVER: What news do you suppose I've just been piping
    From the rooftops?

TOLSON:                      When you pipe I tend
    To fail to listen.

HOOVER:            Marvin Purvis is dead.

TOLSON: As I have just informed you.

HOOVER:                Who told *you*?

TOLSON: Melvin, actually.

HOOVER:           Melvin who, exactly?

TOLSON: Marvin's name was Melvin.

HOOVER:               Morton, Mable,
    Or Melba Toast—how did you get the news?

TOLSON: I've been on the other line.

HOOVER:              With whom?

TOLSON: With Mrs. Purvis.

HOOVER:         Well, you can tell her no.
    Why would I be moved to eulogize
    Some suicidal platter-spinner? No.
    Let him be known as the sometime president
    Of the Carolina Broadcast News Assembly.

TOLSON: She had a request.

HOOVER:           When's the funeral?

TOLSON: She asks that you not attend the service, Jay.

HOOVER: . . . I only asked when it was.

TOLSON:              Tomorrow at three p.m.

HOOVER: . . . How did she find our number?

TOLSON:             His memo book.

HOOVER: He kept my private number all his life?

TOLSON: . . . Get back from there, Jay, have a care.

HOOVER: I am at home. Here I make no bones.

TOLSON: You've been gamboling past the open view
    Like a helium-bloated parade animal.

HOOVER: Do you have the *Post* on the phone, as I requested?
      I want no mention made of Dillinger!
      Or Baby Face or Pretty Boy or Cutie
      Pie or Pooh the Bear or—infants' icons!
      Clyde, have you seen the wrestlers in Mexico?—
      And all these gangsters wore personae like
      The Mexican wrestlers do—Clyde, we must get
      Immediately half a dozen fearful
      Masks from Mexico, and you and I
      Shall wrestle.
TOLSON:               Mexico is in the mirror,
      Should you care to look. Let me get your suit.
HOOVER: When I was a lad, we played cops and robbers.
      Purvis and his gangsters shot it out
      Across the landscape, but, Clyde, by and large
      They played cops and robbers. *We* fight *wars*.
      Our enemies are ideologies,
      And we must smash the vessels that purvey them,
      And not just this one or that one—all of them:
      Black or Communist or Ku Klux Klan,
      All are rationales for disorder,
      All are threats to peace and order,
      All will wax to a size to challenge
      Eventually authority and justice—
TOLSON: John—John—John—John—John—
      John, the temple is going to burst asunder.
HOOVER: And talk to *The New York Times*. The pinko
      shits.
TOLSON: The vein is standing out all blue and ropy—
HOOVER: *The Jew York Times*, more like it.

TOLSON:                          Let's not start.

HOOVER: The goose step is unattractive, I concede,
       But in the man's defense—what now?

TOLSON: To bring your pressure down . . . Take two . . .
       Get dressed.

HOOVER:          Patriotism, vision, strength,
       Consistency and elegance of concept—

TOLSON: Please, Jay, not the Hitler diatribe—

HOOVER: Do we draw across the face of these fine values
       Sort of a black veil because a tragic villain
       Happened to possess them? I refuse.

TOLSON: I love you.

HOOVER:          Yes, the pinstripe double-breasted.
       The goose step is both ominous and silly,
       I warrant, but in the man's defense, he didn't
       Invent the goose step . . .

TOLSON:                          John . . . I love you, John.

HOOVER: . . . HITLER INVENTED THE TWENTIETH
       CENTURY!
       He instituted the control of guns.
       We need such a law ourselves, do we not?
       May I point out that whereas the Negro may have
       To swim up waterfalls to cast a vote,
       He nevertheless may purchase firearms?

TOLSON: Suck in. Zip up.

HOOVER:          BRING ME THE OBITUARY
       OF MARTIN LUTHER KING.

TOLSON:                          Suck *in* your *gut*.
       You have a two p.m. appointment with
       Senator Johnson.

HOOVER:                          Senator LBJ

From Cowturdania. Him a good ol' boy.

TOLSON: He's set aside half an hour for you.

HOOVER: How would you like to see me double that?

One call and his whole afternoon is mine.

He'll drop the German chancellor for me.

TOLSON: He owes you favors.

HOOVER:                          He owes me more than favors.

Bring me a deck of cards. —We'll play gin rummy!

—In our underwear!

TOLSON:                          But I don't play gin rummy.

HOOVER: Not you and I! The senator and I!

He'll play rummy with me if that's my pleasure,

And in his undershorts, if that's my pleasure.

But I think I'll save that game for the Oval Office,

And play it with the president half-naked.

TOLSON: With Eisenhower? Does he fancy cards?

HOOVER: With LBJ, after he takes the White House.

TOLSON: Will LBJ be president one day?

HOOVER: What earthly circumstance would stay the man?

Cremation, and his ashes on the wind.

Go fish. He's got a really enormous dick.

We'll have a round of crazy eights if I

Decree it.

TOLSON:          An enormous what?

HOOVER:                          Shlazool.

Often he pulls it out to drive a point home.

"Mao's got China but he ain't got nuthin' lack 'is."

TOLSON: Has Elvis Presley become the president?

HOOVER: And Eisenhower! —chrome-dome imbecile.

Unless he's reading from a page the man's
Aphasic. Now we've given him a button
He can push to set off World War Three.

TOLSON: An awesome power. He—

HOOVER:                          It doesn't work.

TOLSON: It doesn't—doesn't—

HOOVER:                          Doesn't do a thing.
Push it all day long, he won't succeed
In summoning a shoeshine.

TOLSON:                          Well!—

HOOVER: What do you take us for? The button's phony.
When is supper? Should I be home for supper?

TOLSON: You are persona non grata.

HOOVER: What are we having?

TOLSON:                          Grated persona non grata.
—Jay, back. —First in costume, now half-naked.

HOOVER: They don't know me.

TOLSON:                          Only that you live here,
Only that the windows of Director
Hoover's Georgetown mansion wink
With images of a runaway mannequin.

HOOVER: How will my obituary read?
"Hoover was a fascist bureaucrat, a spy
For Adolf Hitler, shredder of the Bill of Rights"—
And that's if I succeed. But if I fail:
"Hoover let the tendrils of a cancer
Flourish in the very neck of God and choke him
To death."

TOLSON:          I guess you're meaning communism.

HOOVER: "Hoover in silk kimono and garish paint!"

What does it matter? The earth swallows us all.
Behold Melvin Purvis: who led a life,
Who strove, triumphed, prospered, failed, declined,
And perished, and tomorrow at three p.m.
Rejoins the elements; and the same awaits
The ones he left to mourn him,
All of us forgotten in the dirt.
—Where's my Marcus Aurelius? Where's my Marcus
    Aurelius?
I must read him every morning, a few lines—
"Hoover with his secret files and blackmail!"

TOLSON: Crying out for Marcus Aurelius
    As for a slave.

HOOVER:          And in my history
    I want no mention made of Dillinger.
    I will not stand to have the *Post* cry down
    The roll of dust-bowl tommy-gunner rubes.
    "Pretty Boy," "Machine Gun," "Baby Face,"
    "Legs" and "Dutch" and "Bugsy." Dillinger.
    This suit's too blue.

TOLSON:          Too late. The black wingtips—

HOOVER: Nelson killed one of ours at Lake Geneva,
    And again, in his final fight, he took two more.
    They shot him to pieces, but he left them dying
    And stole their vehicle and drove away.
    A beast. He never marked a difference
    Between manslaughter and the wringing of
    A dinner chicken's neck. And Dillinger!
    The spawn of the ungodly partnering
    Of our press's sideshow cynicism

And that gawking yokel, the American soul.
What's this!

TOLSON:　　　　Your nitroglycerin, m'lord.

HOOVER: "Baby Face Nelson." I saw his face. His face
Was not a baby's even in infancy.
I saw him laid out nude and green and pocked
With bullet wounds like small blue mouths.
Before or since I've never looked on death,
Not even Mother in the mortuary,
Only the runty scofflaw Baby Face.
He had the barrel belly and stick limbs
Of a starved Iowa farmer. I wouldn't doubt
He'd chomped his share of dust behind the plow.
. . . Look, Clyde—do you think a clown in costume
Carries no soul inside him, do you think
I'm not a vessel which, when tipped, pours out
The oil of compassion in the beading dirt?
I am a cake of ash surrounding solar
Lusts and molten agonies. Gangsters?
Whatever I arrest them for I've done in *here*.
Whatever their desire drives them to,
Wherever this terrible engine guides or goads them,
I stand there waiting. —Marcus Aurelius!
Hear this, hear this:
"Everything is banal in experience, fleeting in duration,
　　sordid in content; in all respects the same today as
　　generations now dead and buried have found it to be."
Here—you—read on, read on—

TOLSON: "A little while, and all that is before your eyes now will
　　have perished. Those who witness its passing will go

the same road themselves before long; and then what
will there be to choose between the oldest grandfather
and the baby that dies in its cradle?"

HOOVER: Behold Melvin Purvis!—
Squeezed through the story of a life as from
One end and out the other of a python;
And thence to fertilize the graveyard grass—
To feed the thatch of corpses' houses.

TOLSON:                                              This one.

HOOVER: Too red!

TOLSON:              It matches.

HOOVER:                        Red is not my color!

TOLSON: . . . There. You're beautiful. —Now wash it down.

HOOVER: Purvis, Dillinger, lying in your graves:
Assemble your eyeballs from your dead dust to watch
J. Edgar Hoover swallow dynamite!


BLACKOUT

# SCENE 3

*February 29, 1960: A fathomless void.*

*A* MAN *in blood-soaked robe and pajamas, his head
exploded.*

*A* VISITOR *in casual street attire.*

MAN: You, sir! —What do you think you're doing here?

VISITOR: Me? Hanging around. Hovering, more like it.

MAN: Explain your presence, please. You're in my home.

VISITOR: Do you refer to a "house"?

MAN:                                    I do. This house.

VISITOR: There's nothing here but you and me.

MAN:                                              Again
        I ask, and one last time—before I act.

VISITOR: Well, I'll be damned! I recognize you now.

MAN: Of course you do, unless you've burgled us
        At random. State your business, sir, at once.

VISITOR: You're Melvin Purvis, G-man—"Senior" G-man.
        Hero of cereal box and radio.
        The man who collared Dillinger.

PURVIS:                                    And you?

VISITOR: I'm Dillinger.

PURVIS:            John Dillinger?

DILLINGER:                                    The same,
      The chap you collared.
PURVIS:                            So! —A lunatic.
DILLINGER: I'm not the one with the forty-five in his hand
      Wearing his brain for a hat.
PURVIS:                                Am I dreaming?
DILLINGER: This is a dream, but you're not the one who's
      dreaming.
      I am dreaming that you've shot yourself.
PURVIS: Stupid nonsense.
DILLINGER:               Take a look. That's you.
PURVIS: There's never been a mirror there before.
DILLINGER: I've never had a dream like this before.
PURVIS: I don't look well.
DILLINGER:            If you ain't dead, I'd guess
      You hover between the first and second worlds.
PURVIS: And you? Your gravestone says you're dead.
DILLINGER:                                      But
         dreaming.
PURVIS: So—which of us is dreaming?
DILLINGER:                        I'm the one
      Who's dreaming. You're the one who shot himself.
PURVIS: The thing was jammed, I merely tried—
DILLINGER: The automatic forty-five's beloved
      Above its use and quite above its worth.
PURVIS: And where does this dreaming take place? Are you in
      Heaven,
      Or Hell, or some such afterworld, and dreaming?
DILLINGER: No, I'm in Portland, Oregon.

PURVIS:                              I see.

DILLINGER: On Revolution Drive, west of the seventh
        Tee of the Curtis Forest Country Club.
        Do you golf? —I mean, when you have a head?
        I'm not a member, but I love the greens.
        Magenta in the twilight, silvery
        And silken in the dew of dawn. Two cocktails
        Down the hatch at three each afternoon,
        Chuckling at the cavalcade of duffers
        Whanging their pikes awhile, and then I nap;
        And visit the dead in my dreams, apparently.

PURVIS: You're the one who's dead!

DILLINGER:                          O no, not I.
        On July twenty-second, 1934,
        You and your agents, at the Biograph
        Theater on Lincoln in Chicago,
        Ambushed Jimmy Lawrence.

PURVIS:                          Jimmy Lawrence.

DILLINGER: Sort of a guy I kind of knew but didn't
        Like. My Anna fed him to you. Me?
        I was already in Portland.

PURVIS:                          Jimmy Lawrence.

DILLINGER: You asked for Johnny and she brought you Jimmy.

PURVIS: O yes, the whore, the madam, Anna—

DILLINGER:                                Sage.

PURVIS: Your Judas paramour. I *thought* I smelled a rat.

DILLINGER: You wanted a rat. She brought you the cheese.
        Remember: Judas is always working for Jesus.

PURVIS: And I assume you go by—

DILLINGER:                    Jimmy Lawrence!

PURVIS: Balderdash! I saw John Dillinger
      Lying in the grease. I saw him jerking
      Like a frog and then I saw him stop.

DILLINGER: Portland's nice. It has a kind of rainy
      Charm and not a lot of auto traffic.
      I found a lovely lady there I've lived with
      Almost twenty-five years. She's got two kids—
      That is, they're grown now, out of the house,
      But I was pretty well the dad who raised them
      Since they were tots. And do you know, one day
      In 1936 I watched the younger boy
      Rip the top from his box of Post Toasties
      And dump them in a mixing bowl and comb
      His fingers through the flakes and come up with
      —What do you imagine he came up with?

PURVIS: A Melvin Purvis Junior G-man badge.

DILLINGER: The head of your own division! Thanks to me
        Your name shines on.

PURVIS:                          I wasn't seeking fame
      Or power. Only to steer our youngsters toward
      The love of right.

DILLINGER:                  I could have revealed myself—
      Letters to the press, mailed in the dead of night—
      I could have grimed you with humiliation.

PURVIS: And why didn't you?

DILLINGER:                  Well, the legend.
      Jimmy Lawrence possessed a larger-than-life
      Quality, shall we say, which history
      Has tattooed with the name "John Dillinger."

PURVIS: O. The outsized . . . legend.

DILLINGER:                          How's the noggin?

PURVIS: Gives no discomfort at all. Damn this pistol!

DILLINGER: Legend will have it it's the very gun
          You shot me with.

PURVIS:                          It was a gift. I just received it.
          In any case, the night you died I never
          Fired once.

DILLINGER:          With all those barrels blazing
          It's a wonder they didn't drill some innocent.
          Other than Jimmy, of course.

PURVIS:                               Blast this thing!
          I had a tracer round in here, and it was jammed—

DILLINGER: Felled by the gun that made you famous.
               There's irony to the plan.

PURVIS:                                    You've no idea.
          I really cannot conjure a circumstance
          More absurdly ironic than that my head
          Should be skewered by a blazing tracer.

DILLINGER: A private joke?

PURVIS:                     Identify yourself!
          Who are you, sir, and what's your purpose here?

DILLINGER: I just explained all that. I'm Dillinger,
          My mama's favorite. Your head's not working
          Too efficiently, I'd guess.

PURVIS:                          My head!

DILLINGER: It's me, your shining moment—Dillinger.
          . . . Nervous, Purvis?

PURVIS:                     You! —Get out of my house.

DILLINGER: Is it?

PURVIS:          Is it, is it—

DILLINGER:               Is it your house?

     Then offer me a glass of water. Fetch

     Me one of your golf clubs. Touch one thing at all.

PURVIS: I hazard to say we've got a floor beneath us.

DILLINGER: The floor of what?

PURVIS:                         My home. Upstairs. That is—

DILLINGER: This isn't a floor. It's just a more substantial

     Darkness underfoot. If we were breathing,

     I'd say we were sucking on a vacuum.

     But we're not breathing. Airless dream.

PURVIS:                              Assassin!

DILLINGER: Excuse me? What did the pot just call the kettle?

PURVIS: I fought on the side of the law.

DILLINGER:                    The law is a whore.

     You chased men down and killed them in the streets

     And you and I were brothers in our fame.

PURVIS: Fame and infamy are different things.

DILLINGER: They're different words.

PURVIS:                         A bad man's mind

     Troubles itself to slice at the semantics.

DILLINGER: I was a killer and you were a killer too.

     I look at your exploded head and think:

     Now there is the face of justice.

PURVIS:                         What do you mean?

DILLINGER: Come now. I've studied very carefully

     The accounts of the death of Pretty Boy Floyd.

PURVIS: . . . I agree life's not what I thought it was.

     I saw a world divided into shining light

And stinking darkness, saw it as a clash
Of hammer on rock, clash of army on army.
But it's much more beautiful than that.
I've used many years to think on this, I—
Stand back! What are you doing in my house?

DILLINGER: I told you. And I told you that I told you.
You don't recall, because we're moving backwards
Swiftly as you head away from your death.

PURVIS: Why would I be hurtling backwards, sir?

DILLINGER: That's what happens at the end of it all.
A kind of boomerang effect. You slam
Against your finish, carom back toward the start.
Does the name John Dillinger mean anything?

PURVIS: Mean anything! I might as well have married him.
Our names are certainly joined . . . Who might you be?

DILLINGER: As a matter of fact, I am John Dillinger.

PURVIS: Poppycock! Where are we, incidentally?

DILLINGER: Baby Face, Machine Gun, Pretty Boy,
You got 'em all. All but Dillinger.

PURVIS: You don't impress me as the gangster sort.
You hardly seem insane or stupid enough.
It takes a kind of hideous idiocy
To make an outlaw.

DILLINGER:                    What it takes is jizz.

PURVIS: My wife is in this house, sir. Bring your tongue
To heel.

DILLINGER:      Above all what it takes is youth.
Young blood blazing up like gasoline
And a mind that marches in a pounding swoon

To the anthem of its own bubbles.

I knew I wasn't cut out to be a crook.

I knew from the night of my first and only gunfight.

PURVIS: Star Lake.

DILLINGER:          Star Lake, Wisconsin, at the inn.

The place surrounded, bullets in the air,

Corpses hanging out the windows—

For Baby Face it was an opera.

PURVIS: He was a special kind of psychopath.

DILLINGER: Not to say I'd wash my history

Entirely spotless. After the fireworks

An uneventful life feels full to burst.

The front porch swing swings sweeter underneath

A man who's swum through blood to get to it.

Baby Face was how old when he died?

PURVIS: He died young.

DILLINGER:          And lucky he wasn't younger.

Now—tell me how you murdered Pretty Boy.

PURVIS: . . . If you actually happen to be John Dillinger,

If this is an actual conversation in my house,

If this is something other than a dark

Senility I've wandered into dying,

Do you dream I'd come here carrying my sins

To lay at your feet? In any case, I'm clean.

DILLINGER: You ambushed Jimmy Lawrence in an alley

And Pretty Boy was stretched out wounded when

You told a cop to blow his brains away.

PURVIS: I'm satisfied I've chosen the good and the right

In essence.

DILLINGER:     Essence! Now who takes his razor
        To the words?
PURVIS:             In my most human essence, in
        My freedom, where my human gist resides,
        In that freedom God put out of reach
        Even of his own fingertips,
        There is where I choose and where I'm judged.
        I am not a mystery to myself.
        . . . But I seem to have gotten turned around in all
        This darkness . . . Have I committed suicide?
DILLINGER: No. You've had an accident.
        Do you know who you are?
PURVIS:                             I'm Melvin Purvis.
DILLINGER: Correct. The man who collared Dillinger.—
        Before you ask: I'm Dillinger, I'm quite
        Alive, this is a dream, it's not your dream,
        It's my dream, you have blown your head off,
        And you're following it into the afterworld.
PURVIS: And I'm meeting you on the road to the afterworld
        Because I had a hand in your dying?
        Do you offer to guide me down? Or do you stand as
            obstacle?
DILLINGER: You weren't responsible for my death.
        I'm very much alive.
        I'm napping on my porch in Portland, Oregon.
PURVIS: I have a headache!
DILLINGER: You just shot yourself.
PURVIS: Ah! Yes! —And have I committed suicide?
DILLINGER: No. You've had an accident.

PURVIS:                                    You see!
    It isn't what I do that counts; it's why.
    It isn't what I've done; it's what I meant.
    It isn't how I act, but only how
    I'm thinking while I'm acting— Yes, I know,
    It terrifies the heart to learn that good
    And bad come down to infinitely
    Subtle motions of the will, but I've
    Used many years to think on this, I, I—
    ... WE JUST COLLARED DILLINGER!
    This puts our division on the map!
    We had him in the alley. I said,
    "Drop it, Johnny," I said, "we've got you covered."
    He turned, unfurled his coat, went for his gun.
    Hollis opened fire, the others too.
    I never even flicked my safety off.
    He dropped like a puppet with his strings cut.
    Dead before he hit the grease!
    I have a headache!
    Get out of my dream!
    Last night I saw Director Hoover
    Gloating over my death, dressed as a woman,
    Perched like a black crow above my grave.
DILLINGER: And did you read your epitaph on the stone?
PURVIS: Who are you?
DILLINGER:               I told you. You forgot.
PURVIS: I've used centuries to think on this—
DILLINGER: What centuries?
PURVIS:                              The centuries I've wandered
    Through this labyrinth with half a head . . .

[DILLINGER *fades from view.* PURVIS *alone in the void.*]
Lay the cinder of your life across
From mine on the balance, and you'll see which rises.
Witness the consolations of faith—
DILLINGER'S VOICE:                              You're dead!
Where's God? In death it just goes on: still less
And less of anything and more of nothing.
We are the gods, immortal, helpless infants
Watching our minds paint themselves on blackness.
PURVIS: Liar! . . . Demon!
          . . . Whom do I have the honor of addressing?


BLACKOUT

# SCENE 4

*Spring 1959: An office at KSBC radio, Florence, South
Carolina.*

> PURVIS *and* JOB INTERVIEWER, *both in business attire.
> Occasionally we hear the mooing of cows outside.*

PURVIS: Coffee . . .

INT:                    I'm sorry! I'll pour you—

PURVIS:                              Don't bother, it's
       fine—

INT: No bother a-tall! I'm just a little—

PURVIS:                              Oops.

INT: I'll wipe that—God!—here—

PURVIS:                      Not your handkerchief!

INT: That's what it's for!

PURVIS:                  All right, I'll have another—

INT: I'm just a little nervous, shall we say.

PURVIS: But I'm the one who's seeking the position.

INT: Mr. Purvis, you're a man of character.

PURVIS: Thank you, sir.

INT:                      And we are out of cream.
      I feel we're lacking.

PURVIS:                  Not at all. Black's fine.

INT: *I'm* sugar and cream. I feel a certain lack!

   . . . It must have been something, fighting those evil
      gangsters.
   Happy . . . no doubts . . . evil versus good . . .
   To be able to see it all as black or white.
PURVIS: I believe that's what it is. Don't you?
INT: I don't know. Sometimes it *looks* to be,
   But isn't that a sort of gift
   Of circumstance or something, circumstance,
   When right and wrong come clear?
PURVIS:                     I think it's the world.
INT: And other times, though? Aren't some people forced
   Beyond unbearably beyond for instance
   I don't know. Sometimes, to jump on any
   Means for stealing satisfaction from
   This harlot earth, it just about feels sensible.
   Or anyway it sort of sometimes I don't know.
   I shouldn't talk. The dirty harlot world
   Has never stressed my character or tried
   My soul with anything more than office supplies.
PURVIS: And did you withstand the test?
INT:                      I paid them back.
PURVIS: We start off seeing black and white. But then
   We mix the two and things get murky, don't they?
INT: But that's what I mean, I mean, they're here to use,
   For me to use, and so I lug some home,
   Because I work at home, you see, sometimes,
   So it's not who or where but *how* you use
   A stapler or—you see how it gets tricky
   Just by being stuff don't hardly count,
   Just nickels from the coffee fund to plink

For Coca-Cola, which is practically
The *same* as coffee, only colder, till
A three-cent stamp grows complicated and
This feeling grabs you that you're *doing* something,
Something, yes, murky. —Come to murk:
My daddy used to give this lecture where
He'd talk of cleaning up our insides, pouring
The clarity of goodness over the bilge
And swill—well, *you* know, kind of like you'd lavish
Good water into a glass of dirty water?—
Until we're filling up and spilling over?—
And just keep pouring till we stand there clean?
And then God lifts us to his lips, I guess . . .

PURVIS: I'm sorry—your daddy was a lecturer?

INT: At almost every opportunity!
He doesn't lecture quite so much these days.

PURVIS: He's still living?

INT:                                     Bless his soul, I think
He is, barely! . . . How'd we get on *this*?
—At least the ice is busted anyways!
Soun' like time to crack this li'l ol' flask!

PURVIS: Would that reflect too wisely on my efforts
To land employment here at—

INT:                                          Efforts? Heck,
As far as I'm concerned, the job is yours.
I don't have *final* say, but pretty doggone
Near to that, and I say: "Hire the man
Who collared Dillinger."

PURVIS:                               Again: I thank you, sir.

INT: Ludicrous you should even interview.

PURVIS: I'm glad to do it.

INT:                     Fair is fair,
      We might as well see every applicant,
      But we won't see a better—no, you're welcome—
PURVIS: Thank you.

INT:                 Yes. You're welcome.
      . . . Mr. Purvis, just this very morning
      I poked around—my kid's got this old lunch box,
      Old box full of odds and ends, his wealth:
      A beat-up Hohner brand harmonica,
      A half a pliers—you know, just one, just one
      *Plier* you know . . . rocks that must have winked
      Beside the crick, but dried off they're just dull,
      Doodads, thingums, hoojiemajiggers, *stuff*,
      Which I was stirring my curious nosy finger
      Around amongst, and just you look at this.
PURVIS: You don't say!

INT:                 Lodged among the whatnots.
PURVIS: How on earth did he come by such a thing?
INT: That there is mine. I am a Junior G-man.
PURVIS: You mean in thirty-six, I guess, or thirty—
INT: Back when I was a—yep, in thirty-seven.
      Must be—twenty-some-odd—twenty-what—
PURVIS: Delivered from the dark, devouring—
INT:                                         I
      Was quite an admirer or something.
PURVIS:                                 The swarm of
      days.
      A Melvin Purvis Junior G-man badge.
INT [*British accent*]: "Against the gangs of thugs who terrorize

America's prairie states in the 1930s—
Blood-blind murder-mongers with a thirst
For roadhouse hootch and hungering for cash,
Writing their names in America's headlines
With bullets from their tommy guns—against
These outlaw cutthroats ONE MAN STANDS TALL—
A G-man's G-man and a he-man's he-man,
Melvin Purvis, dedicated agent
Of Uncle Sam's new law-enforcement army,
The Federal Division of Investigation,
Later to become the FBI."

PURVIS: Remarkable.

INT:                       Remarkable . . . indeed.
They showed a rousing good short subject all
About you in a theater in London—
Or, anyways, about the FBI.

PURVIS: . . . And you saw London.

INT:                                 I saw France. I saw
Big Ben, the Eiffel Tower, also watched
Bavaria from a train after the war.
Snapshots of a land defeated passing . . .
Yep. I fished it from the cereal.
"Melvin Purvis Junior G-man Corps."
I was quite an admirer of—you.
I didn't know who Melvin Purvis *was*,
Or what he *did*, I just assumed you were
The emperor of all the G-men—well,
I found out later on—the history,
You wouldn't even call it history,
I mean it seems so fresh and so alive,

And even to this day, John Dillinger
And Legs and Dutch and Bugsy, names
Like Pretty Boy, Machine Gun, Baby Face . . .
And I was a Junior G-man and believed
That Melvin Purvis was our king.

PURVIS:                                    O, no,
Not king. The king was Hoover. Was and is.
The king of the G-men, lord of the Junior G-men,
Generalissimo of all the girls
In the Special Junior G-man Girls' Division;
We all were the trembling subjects of J. Edgar,
Immortal Emperor of Is and Was.

INT: And, Mr. Purvis, what of Baby Face?
Didn't I read somewhere you caught him, too?

PURVIS: I wasn't present at his capture.

INT:                                    Was he
Captured?

PURVIS:          He was killed. He fought it out.

INT: I'd be honored if I could work with you.
I'll do everything I can. I'll go to bat
With all my might and see what we can do.

PURVIS: I'll be pleased and grateful if
With all your might you'll see what you can do.

INT: I rose no higher than the junior echelon.
. . . ONE MAN STANDS TALL.

PURVIS:                                    Remarkable.
. . . You went to war?

INT:                          Yes. No. I *went*, I mean—
The European theater—but never
Witnessed or experienced actual—

Participated in *hostilities*—
I have a marksman's badge. It's not a medal,
Just a, just a badge. For hitting targets.
PURVIS: I never went to war but there:
In Illinois . . . Wisconsin . . . In Ohio
Pretty Boy Floyd lay down in a field and died,
Not like an outlaw monster but like any
Baffled youngster with a punctured belly,
Died as I imagine he might have died
In service of his country, that's to say
I saw the same expression in his eyes
I would have seen if we two had enlisted
And shipped for France together at eighteen
Like some of the boys I went to high school with,
And he'd got shot beside me, and I'd held
His fingers and talked happy while the mud
Engrossed him. No, I never saw a war,
But I saw something real.
INT: Good God.
PURVIS:            . . . You read the account?
INT:                              I didn't read—
PURVIS: Recently the officer present says
At my behest he dispatched Charles A. Floyd
With a bullet to the head while Floyd lay helpless.
At my express command.
INT:                              That's damnable!
PURVIS: It would have been if I had done.
INT:                              I mean
To *say* a thing like that! It's scandalous.
PURVIS: So long as what he claims is false.

INT:                                    But say!
        He stains your name!
PURVIS:                        Unless, of course,
        He tells the truth.
INT:                    He tells a goddamn lie!
        Excuse the color of my speech! But say!
        —But coming back to black and white: the notion
        *This* one inhabits goodness, *that* one's veins
        Beat with Satan's blood, I mean—
PURVIS:                                All right,
        Of course the certainty drains slowly away.
        It's as if the battleground surfaces from the ocean
        Of gore and the droplets drain from the faces and then
        What you have are silly Midwestern boys
        And arrogant men with badges on our breasts.
        . . . My qualifications as a broadcaster—
INT: You pick it up in two, three weeks. I did.
        Fact is I studied with an eye on law.
        Went to the local college, just three years.
        That college right there . . .
PURVIS:                        O! Right there! Ah—
INT: A feller couldn't get more local than that!
PURVIS: I thought it was a—sanitarium,
        A lunatic's retreat, or lazar house.
INT: Ha-ha-ha-ha, isn't that a place
        For pestilential leper sorts of folks?
        A lazar house?
PURVIS:            Yes. That is, it looks—
INT: No, a college—well, it *used* to be
        A mental hospital, but ever since

I've known of it, it's been the Baptist college.
Say now, what on earth's the difference?
Either one, you'd have to be crazy to go there.

PURVIS: O, now—

INT:                    Ha ha ha ha ha ha ha.
. . . You wonder about the kids: how do they choose—
I didn't know where to head for, so one day
I walked in through that door and interviewed,
Right like you right now. That was a turn in the road.
Prelaw . . . I almost tried philosophy . . .
I nearly majored in theology.
I was drawn to it because . . . I feel a lack.
I missed my call, I reckon. Yes, right there
I reached a turn in the road. Do you have children?

PURVIS: Children?

INT:                    Yes.

PURVIS:                              —For goodness' sake, of course,
You got me thinking. Yes. I have three sons,
All grown up and on their own. And you?
. . . O, yes, the— Sorry, yes, the . . . lunchbox.

INT: I swore I wouldn't do this, Mr. Purvis,
But I have actually brought the original—
Would you do me the honor of an autograph?

PURVIS: "Official Bulletin from Melvin Purvis!"
       Thanks—I've got a—sure—I'll—thanks—

INT:                                             Use mine!
"A special greeting to all Junior G-men!"
. . . "Purvis"—that's like "Elvis."

PURVIS:                              I'm not Elvis.

INT: Elvis Presley.

PURVIS:        Yes. I know, the—

INT:                            The—

PURVIS: Hillbilly singer.

INT:               Gosh. I'm talking crazy.
     I'm just so nervous. Right—I do have kids.
     . . . "In the days when I was a Junior G-man . . ."
     "Confidential from Melvin Purvis." Well—
     It's sort of an intoxicating honor,
     I mean to me you're big, as big as Elvis
     Would be to my—I have a son, a daughter . . .

PURVIS: Elvis Purvis!

INT:               Ha ha ha ha ha . . .
     Young women mystify and terrify me.
     Have you seen the way they wear those peasant blouses,
     And they pull the elastic down to expose their white
     And mystifying and terrifying shoulders?

PURVIS: Ha ha ha ha ha.

INT: Elvis Purvis, ha ha ha ha ha.
     . . . Is it true that Dillinger, you know, had
     A monstrous, you know, had a monstrous—

PURVIS:                             Yes.
     In an attempt to minister to his wounds
     They cut his clothing from him in the van
     As I was watching. Never such a one
     On any human being. There was gathered
     All the animal evil in him, coiled
     And burgeoning.

INT:               I see. I shouldn't—well.
     —I am that very ordinary bird called
     The Carolina Pot-gut Button-popper.

Middle-aged old rooster with his wings clipped.
Tell the truth I wouldn't be surprised
One morning if I laid a egg! Rr-rr
Rr-roo! My wife thinks I'm a clumsy oaf.
I'm no longer the graceful oaf she married.
. . . Never a G-man. Naught but a Junior G-man.
I haven't got what it takes to be a G-man.

PURVIS: Now, now, you were what? —Eight? Seven?

INT: Seven or eight, I guess—

PURVIS:                                    *Yes*, you were *young*,
You did your very best, I'm sure you made—

INT: I licked the bottom drops of my resolve—

PURVIS: Made every effort—

INT:                                    Every, yes, I did—

PURVIS: Made every effort conceivable in a boy,
A child of seven or eight—

INT:                                    I'm still a child.
. . . O, I had that pamphlet memorized!
"Tips for shadowing suspects." "Secret codes."
"About disguises." "How to surround a house."
Sometimes I feel, do you ever feel, I feel
At night as if my own house is surrounded.
The nights don't give me my rest like they should.
I'm startled awake by noises that aren't there.
I hear the wind, and I can feel the night
Lying over everything.
I can smell the ashtrays in the rooms.
I listen to my wife's breathing,
And sometimes it stops for long intervals,
Sometimes I count as high as eighteen, twenty,

Then she takes a breath. And I realize:
O, my Lord, I'm actually going to die.
Someday these thoughts will end—
I roll out of bed in terror and I fall
To my knees beside the bed
And I call out for anything at all
To hear me, and I shape a clear resolve
And whisper vows that come as feverish
As any I would make to get the hangman's
Noose from off my neck. But I don't know
What, exactly, I'm promising, *some*thing, just
Some way of being different, and if I *can*,
Then that will save the world . . . But I don't know . . .
The nights don't give me my rest like they should.

PURVIS: Are you describing a dream?

INT:                                        Is this a dream?
In the daylight my blood feels watery.
All my vows and all my fine resolves
Dissolve into corruption.
I walk around the town and everything
Feels silent no matter how much noise we make,
Like we aren't *people*, we haven't been *informed*,
We're walking around but we have no names.
I used to enjoy the moving picture shows,
But now I sit there in the crowd and I just
Smell my fellow Americans stinking and
I hear the breath ride in and out of their mouths
So loudly it mutes the spectacle.
Do you remember *Frankenstein* with Boris
Karloff?

PURVIS:       Enervation, lassitude—
INT: I feel like fate has played me for a sucker,
        Sold me a ticket printed on a cobweb—
        Where's the glorious circus? It's dark. I hear the wind.
        It was only a noise in a dream that woke me up.
        There isn't any Heaven. There isn't any Hell.
        I smell the ashtrays in the rooms . . . And then
        I rise from bed. I go into the morning.
        My children embrace me vaguely and politely,
        My daughter comes to kiss me, and her face
        And fingers smell like the puppy she's been petting.
        And in this world the spring is turning green
        And I see how I'm beginning to disappoint
        My son. Just as I disappointed my father.
        What pleased me once no longer pleases me,
        And the bright things pale in my sight,
        And meanwhile, things that never could have failed—
        My little daughter's little hand, her kisses—
        They give out. Give way. And now my daughter
        Stands level with my shoulder, and she wears
        Those peasant blouses, and her friends . . . are pretty.
        And I go to see my father at his house.
        He sits in a wicker chair beside a weeping
        Willow and the chair is chipped and sets
        Askew and he tips a little and his hands
        Are tiny and his fly is down and his eyes
        Are wet and red-rimmed; and the way they shine
        While something works the corners of his mouth,
        He looks as if he's trying not to laugh
        At something terrifying coming up

Behind me. "Dad," I say, and he says, "What,
What is it?"—but the point is gone in saying,
Dad, I'm someone you might pride yourself
To call your son. For all the hope of reaching
Him who was my father, I might as well
Be speaking to his headstone. "Father, Father,
It's raining on us both, on me and on
Your wicker chair beside the weeping willow."
One afternoon when I was a child the sky
Blackened and bits of trash whirled up and around
And the rain ripped down like knives and at the window
Of the house my father held me in the crook
Of his arm, I was that small, and we both watched
That willow twisting till a lash of lightning
Tore a third of it away from the trunk
And pitched it across the yard—and, sir, no storm,
No wind, no dark, no violence
Could possibly have touched me in the fortress
Of my father's arm.
     . . . O well . . . O well . . . Ah, shit. Ah, shit.
Mr. Purvis, I can stride right now
Right into that pasture right out there
And tickle fresh, warm milk from out the teats
Of the great-grandchildren of the very cows
Who gave us milk to pour on our Post Toasties!
     . . . I mean when I was a child. When I was a child.
PURVIS: . . . Yes. The cows out there look very healthy . . .
INT: . . . I spoke too much. I always do. I always—
PURVIS: Let me tell you of the death of Baby Face.
     . . . Remember, now, this bloodgush horrorshow

Unfolds within a splendid natural silence
Forty miles outside Chicago proper,
Near Baker Lake, where the mallard ducks
Had not yet left, though late November had come,
And they sailed on its glass . . . All right:
Two of my agents, Ryan and McDade,
Passing a Ford on the Northwest Highway, matched
Three numbers on its plates with those of Nelson's,
Now America's number one Most Wanted.
They quickly turned around, but so did Nelson,
Absolutely ready for a fight,
And when they crossed again, again he turned,
And chased them north, firing his tommy gun,
Chewing up their car, and they fired back,
Neither drawing blood as yet. With Nelson
Traveled his woman Helen and John Paul Chase,
A red-mouthed harlot and a no-good punk,
And now, as they fell behind, leaking
Water from a punctured radiator,
Two more agents in another car
Closed with Nelson's Ford V-8—Sam Cowley
And Herman Hollis—Nelson chasing agents
And agents chasing Nelson—until Ryan
Sped away, quite unaware that help
Had come. As Nelson's engine quit, he turned
Into the Northside Park in Barrington
And bumped to a halt. Helen ran for a drainage
Ditch and Chase and Nelson grabbed their guns
And ducked behind the Ford and fired at Sam
And Hollis as their car went by. The agents

Bailed, neither wounded, Hollis taking
Cover from his car and Cowley rolling
Into a second ditch, both firing back.
Now, Cowley headed our Chicago office,
And Hollis was with me at the Biograph
When we took Dillinger. Hollis was among
The men who actually shot and killed the varlet.
Crack shots both, firing from good cover,
They gave no quarter in this battle until,
Quite beyond my comprehension to this day,
Nelson simply stood up, steadying
His Thompson at his hip, and strode toward them,
Firing rapid bursts and cursing. Cowley
Hit him in the side, yet he kept coming.
He took another in the belly, still came on,
Rounded the car and slaughtered Hollis as
The agent ran for different cover, and,
Turning to Cowley—who'd been filling him
All the while with bullets—stood above him
There at the ditch's edge and made his wife
A widow with the tommy gun. He then
Managed to get in the federal car and start it,
And then those bastards sped away and left
Two agents, good men both, dead in their wake.
Next morning, in a cemetery close
To Nelson's hometown, Fox Grove, Illinois,
They found his naked corpse wrapped in a blanket.
The coroner counted seventeen bullet holes.
His name was Lester Joseph Gillis. He
Was one week shy of twenty-six years old.

INT: Seventeen, you—seventeen, you say.

PURVIS: No mere human could have lived beyond
 The impact of the first four or five.
 I thought, Now that is what we're up against:
 Psychosis of a power to hold a man
 Aright and marching like some—

INT:                                              Lazarus!—

PURVIS: Indeed, some revenant, some Frankenstein—

INT: Old Boris Karloff!—or the Mummy—

PURVIS:                                              Yes,
 As the bullets fill him—

INT:                                    Saint Sebastian martyred
 By the arrows!—

PURVIS:                        Well, you get the point.

INT: I'm sorry. What a picture, though! Excuse.

PURVIS: His dead flesh animated by the lava
 Of anti-authoritarian disrespect.
 . . . I don't care whose side that man was on,
 In 1918 they'd have borne his coffin
 Draped with glory through the streets of home.

INT: You shouldn't say such things.

PURVIS:                                    It's all
 A mystery.

INT:                 But never say it is.

PURVIS: I never shall again. You have my word.

INT: And you, sir, have a job.

PURVIS:                              I'll strive in it.


BLACKOUT

# SCENE 5

*January 1935: An office of the U.S. Division of Investigation, Chicago.*

*During the scene we sometimes hear the commotion of a nearby elevator.*

HOOVER *behind the desk, dressed in a business suit.*

*He makes faces and clenches his fists and wrings his hands, screams and laughs and weeps—all silently.*

HOOVER [*into intercom*]: . . . Blanche.

BLANCHE'S VOICE: Yes, sir.

HOOVER: Is he still in the anteroom?

BLANCHE'S VOICE: Yes. Mr. Purvis is standing in the anteroom.

HOOVER: What is he doing now?

BLANCHE'S VOICE: He's—standing in the anteroom.

HOOVER: Have you got him by the window? Left side?

BLANCHE'S VOICE: No, sir.

HOOVER: No, sir?

BLANCHE'S VOICE: I told him to stand by the window, but he
    moved.

HOOVER: All right. [*On phone*] Hello.
    I wish to place a person-to-person call—
    Excuse me. Later. I'll—goodbye . . . [*Into intercom*] Now,
    Blanche,

Who is ascending? I hear someone ascending.

That whirring again. That whir and thunk. I hear it.

BLANCHE'S VOICE: They went to another floor.

HOOVER:                                        Quite right. All
right.

Goodbye. [*On phone*] Hello. Hello. Person-to-person,
please,

To the Hoover residence in Washington, D.C.

Temple six eight seven seven eight.

O— Mr. Hoover for Mrs. Hoover. Sorry.

. . . Mother, how are you? . . . Mother, put your mouth

Nearer the mouthpiece; that's why they call it that.

Mother, I miss you . . . It's cold, the rivers are frozen.

This wind will whirl you around and slap your face.

. . . O, I love you too . . . O, I miss you sorely.

How are you doing? . . . How are you doing, Mother?

How are the cats? . . . How are the cats? The—

How does Snooky Snooker snuggle without me?

O, that's sweet! . . . He's precious. So are you.

. . . Mother, I want your prayers today, especially

Today. Go on your knees, dear Mother, and pray

That I find the strength to go about my work.

. . . I know you do, I know you do, but now

As much as ever, Mother . . . Thank you.

. . . There isn't any danger, Mother. I'm just—

. . . O, O, no no no. The telephone—

The telephone can't hurt you . . . No no no,

Chicago telephones are harmless, too.

. . . All right, but never fear. And pray for me.

All right, all right—hello? Hello?—Goodbye.

[*Leaps to his feet.*]

. . . What's this, my man—a hooligan's switchblade knife?

But I am a servant of the law. And yet

I hold this blade, how sharp, and to what purpose?

Huuuuh! Hrrrrrrh! Haah! Hhm-hhm! Hrrraaggghhh!

They said you had a lot of guts! Quite so!

Let me introduce you to your bowels.

Here's the large, and here the small intestine.

My! What have you been eating? —Eat it again!

Hah-HAH hrrr-hrrr HLLL HLLL haaghr AAH.

How do you look in this year's very latest

Fashionable scarf, the tripe-of-traitor

From deep in the interiors of you?

There! Now I'm the man who collared Purvis!

You're trembling, trembling, let me snug your cravat.

How you blush! Too much? O no, I mustn't

Strangle you, no. No, you're going to spend

Seven long days begging to be strangled!

HAAARGH HUUUH huh huh huh huh huh . . .

[*Resumes his seat.*]

. . . Send him in . . . Hhhhrrrr. Hrrrrhh. Hrrrh. Hrrrh.
Hrrrh.

[MELVIN PURVIS *enters.*]

Here's our man, "the man of the hour"! Sit.

PURVIS: Welcome to Chicago, sir.

HOOVER:                            Director.

PURVIS: Welcome to Chicago, Director.

HOOVER:                                  Hoover.

Director Hoover.

PURVIS:                     Welcome to Chicago—

HOOVER: Title and name, Special Agent Purvis.

PURVIS: Welcome to Chi—

HOOVER:                   Thought I'd better see

     Firsthand how things are done in the Windy City.

PURVIS: Well, you're most—

HOOVER:                    The city of the big shoulders,

     Hacker and stacker and mover of meats, O bold

     Encaser of meats, Special Agent Purvis.

     Special Agent Purvis: title—

PURVIS:                  and name,

     Yes, sir—or, yes, Director Hoo—

HOOVER:                  Quite so.

     Marvin, are you hungry? You look hungry.

PURVIS: I believe we're going to lunch? Or am I wrong.

HOOVER: Hark! Our luncheon rises in its cage.

     [*To intercom*] Is that for us, Blanche? —Lunch is on the
         way.

     [*Two box lunches arrive. Meanwhile:*]

     . . . Well. Quite a year. Quite a half-year—

     Five months, more like, what hey? Three villains down.

     Dillinger, Baby Face, and Pretty Boy.

PURVIS: I wouldn't flatter them with monickers.

     Or even names. Nor shrines. Nor histories.

     Not even so much as markers on their graves.

HOOVER: What, then?

PURVIS:            Urinals.

HOOVER:               —Good, Midwestern milk:

     Here's to "the man who collared Dillinger"!

     . . . But we aren't cowboys, are we, sir? Or clowns?

     We can't be turning handsprings, courting headlines.

PURVIS: An officer charges foremost into the fray.
        He can't lead from behind.
HOOVER:                          What luscious ham!
        —*May* I call you Marvin?
PURVIS:                          My name's Melvin.
HOOVER: *I* see. Melvin. Melvin. Melvin's rather . . .
        Swiss cheese, mustard—milk all right?
PURVIS: Yes, Director Hoover.
HOOVER:                          Call me . . .
PURVIS: Edgar? . . . John?
HOOVER:                    Director Hoover will do.
        [*They address their meals. Neither actually succeeds in
            eating anything. Meanwhile:*]
        . . . What do you make of this Adolf Hitler fellow?
PURVIS: He seems a volatile ingredient.
HOOVER: Still and all, don't you think he trains
        His mind with clarity on all the truly
        Modern problems? On the subjugation
        Of growing populations, one might say
        On swollen populations—one might say
        Tumescent throbbing citizenries?
        They must be kept in hand, but ever so gently.
        We can't accomplish this by deadly force
        Of arms. A zealous subtlety is wanted,
        Vigilance, subtlety, creativity.
PURVIS: He strikes me as a dangerous maniac.
HOOVER: . . . Marvin—Melvin? Marvin? Marvin—*Melvin*,
        Help me, please.
PURVIS:                  Of course, Director Hoover.
HOOVER: I'm composing a letter of termination.

PURVIS: Termination? Do you refer to a death?

HOOVER: I don't. I mean the ending of employment.

    . . . We moderns author a language suited to

    Our work: the work of faceless entities.

    The modern age boils slowly forward on

    The inauspicious labors of a multitude,

    Comings and goings, routes and dates and times,

    Bits and pieces, instruments and engines,

    A monstrous undergrowth of pipes and wires,

    And, Marvin, what do you suppose prevents

    The behemoth from strangling on itself?

    Order: tables, lists, charts, graphs,

    Indices, appendices,

    Inventories, catalogues.

    And who shall keep these treasures holy?

    The men of the bureaus; we, the Bureaucrats!

    We who stalk our shadows in the halls,

    We who strum the blades of pages with

    The ridges of our fingerprints. In battle

    We unsheath the alphabet and drive deep

    The Dewey decimal. Quite right—small stuff.

    Yet we accomplish in the aggregate

    What Hercules and Theseus would've—

    Theseus married, as I think you know,

    The queen of the Amazons. I shall never marry.

    I am wife and husband to this work.

    *Bureaucrat.* The word makes music.

    I am having our branch redesignated:

    No more "Division of Investigation."

    Is this a division? —Are we, then, dividers?

No! *Bureau* is the French for "desk":
Our steed, our tank, our Howitzer.
Our battleship! Dreadnought! Gunboat! Bastard
    schooner!
"The Federal Bureau of Investigation."
Yes. A bureau. We'll be Bureaucrats!

PURVIS: Like Jason and the Argonauts.

HOOVER:                              Somewhat.

PURVIS: Hoover and the Bureaucrats.

HOOVER:                              Just so.

[*He gathers both their meals together, and lunch is over.*]
. . . I am holding in my mind the text
Of a lacerating letter to demand
The resignation of a renegade.
Demand, did I say? No. I shall command.
I'll reduce our Mr.—"P"—to pabulum.
But, sir, whereas I taste the very words
Like blood on my tongue, I can't quite redden the page.
O, would you help?
I want somehow to remonstrate and also
Devastate, you see. He must be wounded.
He's grown to quite the prideful peacock,
Fanning and strutting and shimmying, grinding
Under his spurs the faces of his betters.
He's slimy with adulation. It's ungrateful.
—There's the crux, he's just ungrateful, there
You have its full and quivering extent.

PURVIS: You ask me to help you phrase
    The letter of my so-called termination?

HOOVER: I'll settle for a writ of resignation.

PURVIS: You won't get one. Fire me. Put it on paper
　　　　Above your name for all the world to see.

HOOVER: . . . Perhaps I spoke too vigorously just now.
　　　　The hurt of having been outshone, you see,
　　　　The piercing of a beneficiary's
　　　　Ingratitude, you see—that corkscrew works
　　　　Deeper and deeper—*you* see.

PURVIS:　　　　　　　　　　　How can I not?

HOOVER: Vigor of tongue is for the politician.
　　　　We are the new, soft, strong, gray men, in whom
　　　　A kind of soapy equanimity
　　　　Is not entirely uncalled for.
　　　　The proper bureaucrat must keep
　　　　Alert but noncommittal.

PURVIS:　　　　　　　　　　Like a dog.

HOOVER: . . . Have you visited the pyramids of Egypt?
　　　　—But you've seen photos. We could raise a hundred
　　　　In twenty months. A pyramid was called
　　　　"The place where men are turned to gods."
　　　　. . . How do you find Chicago, Agent Purvis?
　　　　Isn't winter like a thousand razors?

PURVIS: It's still autumn.

HOOVER:　　　　　　　And down near zero!
　　　　A million miles from sunny Carolina.
　　　　[*Sings*] *I'd walk a million miles*
　　　　*For one of your smiles*—

PURVIS: And just last month we had a solid week
　　　　Of days that broke a hundred.

HOOVER:　　　　　　　　　Brutal stuff!—
　　　　Brutal.

PURVIS:      I can't tell you what it is,
    But think of all the killers bred from here:
    The Daltons; Frank and Jesse James;
HOOVER: The Youngers;
PURVIS:                    Johnny Ringo,
HOOVER:                              Ringo, really—
    Wyatt Earp grew up in Pella, Iowa,
    As I remember reading—
PURVIS:                    Yes, quite right,
    And Katie Elder came from Davenport.
HOOVER: The vagaries of climate—
PURVIS:                         Or the diet,
    All this dust, the hopeless distances,
HOOVER: The vertigo of horizontal vastness—
PURVIS: The sweet, mild Carolinas don't conduce
    This bloody tommy-gun-style criminal
    Deportment. The hypnotic wheat
    Of Kansas, Illinois, that's where these boys
    Rise out of, and they're mean. They come for blood
    With the innocence of sucklings. Charles A. Floyd
    Hardly blinked, so say the witnesses,
    When he and his accomplices gunned down
    Four noble cops, including one of ours,
    That day at the Kansas City station.
    Killing suited him.
HOOVER:                    Well, killing's what you gave him.
PURVIS: Charles A. Floyd was struck down in the throes
    Of violent resistance to arrest.
    The same for Gillis—alias Baby Face—
    The same for Dillinger.

HOOVER:                 Alias Jimmy Lawrence.

PURVIS: That is not an alias known to me.

HOOVER: I was a guest at City Hall last week.

         Had my photo snapped with Mayor Kelly;

         And he—that is, the mayor—raised the name

         Of Michael Green, the officer on hand

         With you when Dillinger was shot. Mike Green?

         Chicago cop?

PURVIS:          I think it rings a bell.

HOOVER: O, you hear a *bell* ring, do you, Purvis?

         Officer Green, in turn, has raised the name

         Of Jimmy Lawrence—ding dong!—Jimmy Lawrence?

PURVIS: I repeat: The name is not familiar.

HOOVER: . . . All day long I gaze at the faces of liars,

         And to my practiced eye the difference

         Between your face and that of a liar is vast,

         So vast I might be staring into the face

         Of Boris Karloff playing Frankenstein,

         That's how monstrously rare a face you have.

         It's not the face of a liar. I believe the name

         Of Jimmy Lawrence is not familiar to you.

PURVIS: Will you tell me who he is?

HOOVER: You're not a liar, unless, perhaps,

         You work a self-deception practically

         Hallucinatory in its intensity.

PURVIS: I see you launched on your bureaucratic

         Argosy and I no longer view

         Your world as one in which I'm possible.

HOOVER: Hero, what do you accuse me of?

         Cowardice, no—*effeminacy?*—what?

PURVIS: I don't. I've cast no implication here.

HOOVER: The room is ripe with it. A cloying, rotten
      Honey. I can't breathe. Where's a breath?

PURVIS: . . . Never let it be known
      Outside this room I spoke this way;
      But you are false, sir. What you do is a falsehood.
      You are a lie. I want you to understand
      I've lived. You never will. I'll die.
      You'll neither live nor die. You'll simply
      Fade as the truth comes out.
      . . . I can't say what I've fought to save,
      The right things, the good things, the people who hope
        for them,
      But I know what I've fought against,
      I've seen it animate
      The heart of a gangster with seventeen bullets in him,
      And I didn't come here
      To knuckle under to its latest guise.
      You are the Dark, the Death.

HOOVER:                       You want to call me
      Devil—but sophistication robs you
      Of a name for me and leaves you stammering.
      You're so mundane, you're so unworthy, so
      Ignoble in your vision, so one-eyed.
      Don't you see that we shall minister for gods
      That *we* create? We'll don the heads of beasts
      And speak with new tongues, dancing in the smoke
      Of sacrificial fires!—while outside
      The glowing pyramid the multitude
      Feels the pull and trembles and bows down.

I curse you, sir. I raise you high above
The flames and break your body!

*Silhouetted in a purple light,*
*To the rhythms of a sexual, melting jazz*
*Composed in an exotic scale,*
HOOVER *enacts a private rite, making*
*Supplication to the numina*
*Who animate his trembling desires.*

PURVIS *looks on, utterly motionless.*
*And while the light transforms itself around him,*
*He, despite the onslaught of these powers,*
*Undergoes, himself, no transformation.*

BLACKOUT

# SCENE 6

*October 22, 1934: A cornfield near Wellsville, Ohio.*
    *A long shriek of agony . . .*
    *Vast fields at night.*
    PRETTY BOY FLOYD *lies amid rows of stubble. His shrieking subsides.*
    PURVIS *stands right; far left, a uniformed* OHIO STATE HIGHWAY PATROLMAN.
    *Except at the very end,* PURVIS *never once looks in* FLOYD'*s direction.*
    *A meteor shower makes shooting stars. Occasionally one or two or even three at a time streak through the sky.*

PURVIS: How much whiskey could be mashed and dripped
      From all this corn, do you suppose, that is,
      If it were corn, if we weren't standing in a waste
      Of stubble? Half the county could get good
      And cross-eyed. Have a whiskey-mashin' bash.
      Fiddler scrapin' up a waltz, one voice singing,
      Thump of the one-string washtub bass, and the tuba basso
      Too of the jug old Granddad blows across
      The mouth of—oompapa oompapa oompapa—and
      The revelers tromping up from the elderly

Floorboards a sprinkling of oaken dust.
—Oaken? Or alder? What do you build things with
Here in the Midwest, here in the treeless plains,
Out here 'mongst the plowed infinitude?
What are your floors and walls constructed of?
Corncobs? Cornstalks? Mortared with the drool
And cud of cows? If I took you back home
With me to visit, down in South Carolina,
I fear you'd deeply miss this place. You'd anguish
Wretchedly for flatness. You'd tell how
In west Ohio at sunset you can see
Clear across to dawn next Saturday.
But South Carolina's way past Jupiter
Tonight . . . How are you, Pretty Boy?

FLOYD:                              I'm peaches!
Many's the night I've lain all night in the cornrows.
Plenty of times I've tapered off a spree
All ragg'd up and dreaming in the chaff.
You just wind *up* here when the times get jolly!
It's soft as feathers till you get to squirming,
Then it bothers and pokes a feller. Well,
But I won't squirm, because I'm paralyzed,
Because you shot me in the back. My hero!

PURVIS: Oompapa, oompapa, oompapa, oompapa,
There's a little town in Iowa called Lone Tree.
Now, I've been through Lone Tree. And the tree is gone.
Someday the name will be Forgotten Tree.

FLOYD [*sings*]: *The ring-dang-doo, now what is that?*
*It's round and black like a bowler hat.*
*It's good for me, and it's good for you,*

*And it's what they call the ring-dang-doo.*

Now, looky here, I pissed my pants!

PURVIS:                                    That's blood.

FLOYD: Blood! Well, that's all right then.

PURVIS: Charles Arthur Floyd, your life is leaking.

If you've done crimes as yet not laid to you,

You'd best own up and shed the burden.

FLOYD [*sings*]:                                    O,

*When I was a lad not seventeen*

*I met a gal from New Orlean.*

*She had blond hair and eyes so blue*

*And she let me ride on the ring-dang-doo.*

I wish I *had* a few big things to say.

I wish I had a book to read a speech from.

I wish last April this poor dirt-scratcher

Owns this place had plowed the alphabet

Under these rows so all around would stand

Important words. All I can tell you is

The dirt feels natural to lie here dying,

And why so many shooting stars tonight?

PURVIS: Those are meteorites rubbing the air:

Like match heads dragged along the leg

Of dungarees so fast they pop up blazing.

FLOYD: I guess they're bigger than a match head, though.

PURVIS: Smaller, actually. *Popular Mechanics*

Or *Popular Science* had an article.

They're rarely more substantial than a jot

Of sand.

FLOYD:            A little grit makes all this show!

. . . I'd like to tell you things I remember. Damn,

The words get smaller down here at the end.

[*Sings*] *The ring-dang-doo, now what is that*
*It's soft and round like a pussycat*
*It's got a hole in the middle and it's split in two*
*And it's what they call the ring-dang-doo*

PURVIS: The Kansas City station! June last year!

FLOYD: I never did it! By the Devil's luck

I *were* in Kansas City on that day
But never shot nobody, never knew
A word about it! . . . Boys, I swear to you,
Laid out in my maker's lap and looking
Death in the eyes, I swear it.

PATROLMAN:                              Well, he swears.

PURVIS: A villain's oath. Shoot him in the head.

FLOYD: What did he say?

PATROLMAN:              Sir—did you say—

FLOYD [*sings*]: O, *mademoiselle from Armentières,*
        *Parlez-vous*
        *O, mademoiselle from Armentières,*
        *Parlez-vous*

PATROLMAN and FLOYD [*sing together*]:
        *O, mademoiselle from Armentières,*
        *She hasn't been kissed in forty years.*
        *Hinky dinky parlez-vous.*

PATROLMAN: Did you say "Shoot him in the head"?

FLOYD:                                        Aw, naw . . .

PATROLMAN: But you said "Shoot him in the head."

PURVIS:                                    Did I?

PATROLMAN: You heard him say it—didn't you hear him, Floyd?

FLOYD: Aw, he didn't mean it. Naw, you didn't, did you?

. . . "Alouette," that's a right one for ye.
    Would you fellers care to, care to—
    [*Sings*] *Alouette, gentille alouette* . . .

PATROLMAN: I'll shoot him if you say.

FLOYD:                               Seems like the wind
    Blew by and sucked some rain along behind it.

PURVIS: The Kansas City Massacre.

PATROLMAN:                      I know.

FLOYD: I say we'll feel the drops in just a while.

PURVIS: Good men shot down unarmed.

FLOYD:                           I wasn't there!
    [*Sings*] *For half a shilling she'll lay her down*
    *Parlez-vous*
    *For half a shilling she'll lay her down*
    *Parlez-vous*

PATROLMAN *and* FLOYD [*sing together*]:
    *For half a shilling she'll lay her down*
    *She'll jolly well kill ya for half a crown*
    *Hinky dinky parlez-vous*

PATROLMAN: You seem chipper.

FLOYD:                      I ain't shot so bad.
    I've felt worser after Daddy thrashed me.

PATROLMAN: Did you know that one, sir?

PURVIS: I know it, but I don't sing such songs.

FLOYD: I'll tell you a story, since you don't care for songs.
    I'll tell you the story of something that happened one day.
    I hired on a farm one time for getting
    The hay into the barns when I were nine
    Or thereabouts—tall work for any age.
    We scraped from dark till dark eleven days

And didn't pause for Sunday. None but hay:
Cut it, raked it, baled it, hauled it, stacked it,
Breathed it, ate it, and at end of day
Laid down to sleep in it, and by God all
Night dreaming of it too, that itchy, dusty
Hay come up from Hell. So then one day
He says, "Come raking with your hands along
The floor here in the barn and throw them bits
Out in the corral," and we says, "Farmer,
Why?" and he says, "Folks, because you're done—
Look around!" And I raised up my heavy
Eyes and watched the mounds of hay go marching
Off in every way I looked, and underneath
A golden carpet in the slanty afternoon.
He says, "Them as wants to make for Gaithersburg
I'll pay you out, and there's nine miles of road
To take you walking. Them as likes to go
To Millerton the opposite, jump on
Aboard my wagon and I'll haul you." Well,
I rode in the back with my legs a-dangling,
Rode past the mounds, all that we made, and then
Past the mounds on the next farms, that we hadn't made,
And it was so restful to be done,
And then on toward into Millerton.
And I hopped off before the ice cream parlor
And went inside to get me something heaped
High in a bowl, and there I saw my uncle
Who'd lost his eyes, my uncle Charles that took
That blinds-you kind of fever in his cradle:
Now he's blind, and having some dessert.

I never said a word hello. I sat right by
And only watched. I watched him fetch
A ball of ice cream in a sugar cone
And eat it in the most . . . I'm going to find
The word for when you're blind and you eat ice cream.
First you hold the cone and touch it with
Your either fingers, then you hitch your chin
And nose up like you plan to make a speech,
And all you do is smell. And, boys, I think
You listen to it too, I think he heard
The dabs come melting and a-waxing along
The sugar edges of that cone like little
Moons till just that very first sneaked down
And touched his fingers. Then he started;
He tried the drops, the cone, the tippy top
And sides of that ball, and all of it with
The tip, the sides, the under, and the broad
Of his tongue, and every now and then down came
His lips like a babe's over that creamy teat,
And nothing could disturb him. What's the word
For going at an ice cream cone that way?
'Cause then I bought my triple chocolate sundae
For me, and don't you see? I was a child.
And I ate it like a blind man, just as loving,
And when I watched my uncle tasting his,
I watched him like a blind boy who could see.
The word for doing things that way is "young."
The word for that is "young, when you were nine."
It makes me kind of glad that I remember.
It makes me wish you wouldn't kill me, boys.

Boys, right here in this here pocket I've
Got over a hundred and twenty dollars cash.
PURVIS: Tempting us with bribes won't help you, Floyd.
PATROLMAN: Keep your cash.
FLOYD:                              I wasn't trying a bribe!
I only wanted to tell you something nice.
[*Sings*] *Mademoiselle from Armentières,*
*Parlez-vous*
*Mademoiselle from Armentières,*
*Parlez-vous*
*She'll do it for wine, she'll do it for rum,*
*She'll do it for candy or chewing gum!*
You ever see them tracers in the war?
PURVIS: I was never in the war.
FLOYD:                              You never seen
A tracer bullet? Man, they look like comets.
PURVIS: Those are meteors. A comet's quite
Another thing.
FLOYD:                    They look like shooting stars.
PATROLMAN: That's what they are! For golly's sake,
Shooting stars are meteors and falling
Stars are comets!
FLOYD:                    Mares eat oats and does
Eat oats and little lambs eat ivy!—Jeez!
[*Sings*] *The ring-dang-doo, now what is that?*
*It's round and black like a bowler hat.*
*It's good for me, and it's good for you,*
*And it's what they call the ring-dang-doo.*
. . . You know, there ain't no moon tonight.
Nor stars, except them meaty-balls . . . O! Look!

PATROLMAN: . . . Mr. Floyd? Say . . . Pretty Boy?

PURVIS:                                   What's this?

PATROLMAN: . . . O Lord, his brains is spirtled on the corn.
    I think he's shot—he's shot right through his head!
    Who shot him?

PURVIS:             I didn't hear a shot. Did you?

PATROLMAN: I heard no shot. Nor did I shoot him, sir.

PURVIS: Of course not.

PATROLMAN:          Sir, get down. We'd best take
        cover.

PURVIS: . . . By Heaven above, I don't believe such luck.
    This man's been struck in the head by a meteorite.

PATROLMAN: God's bloody stripes! When does that ever
        happen?

PURVIS: Never. I'd say of all the men to die,
    This man's the first to die of a meteor.

PATROLMAN: . . . Mr. Purvis, I'd like to go get drunk.
    Here he lays, the criminal the hobos
    Made a song about, who started off
    A knock-knee spittle-slurper farmer boy
    That couldn't count his toes if he used his fingers,
    And stole a pistol, stole a car, stuck up
    A string of grocers, bought a tommy gun
    And dunked Ohio in a vat of nightmares—
    Slaughtered innocent sucklings at the breast,
    Raped their mothers, killed their fathers—and here
    He lays without a pillow or a dream,
    Assassinated by a shooting star.

PURVIS: Let's get him to the road so we can load him.

PATROLMAN: I'm gonna go get drunk.

PURVIS: His legs . . . His legs . . .
Put your gun away. That's right . . . That's right . . .
Take his legs.
*Soon they find themselves positioned as if staging Caravaggio's* Entombment of Christ.

BLACKOUT

# SCENE 7

*May 1934: A hotel suite on Little Star Lake, Wisconsin.*
    JOHN DILLINGER *and* BABY FACE NELSON: DILLINGER *in casual attire,* NELSON *in shirt, socks, and undershorts, modeling a huge, garish necktie.*
    *In a corner of the room a woman lies facedown, half-naked, bound and gagged.*

DILLINGER: Since when?
BABY FACE:              Since the invention of the wheel.
    Since the invention of fuck.
DILLINGER: Yer just a cracker someone hocked and dripped
    A green-and-yellow speckled loogie on.
BABY FACE: Anyway, is there a law against it?
    Point me in the book where it says a law.
DILLINGER: Sometimes style is all a man has got.
BABY FACE: Style is for the girlies!
DILLINGER:                 Keep that necktie
    Far from populated areas.
BABY FACE: Helen's got a cousin loves this tie.
    Say, *she* ain't a feast and a half for these baby blues!
    A variable Oktoberfest, in fact.
DILLINGER: This vacation has gotta be absolutely
    The final proof that I'm an idiot.

BABY FACE: Hey, let's get over to Oktoberfest.

It's something the Bohemies do, and do

They drink? And get so dead blind sozzled

The girlies almost fuck themselves *for* ya?

DILLINGER: I'd like to pose a query.

BABY FACE: I ain't queerie, dearie.

Listen, John, they even grow beer gardens.

Don't ask me how they do it, but they do.

. . . I'm all ears. Pose as queerly as you want.

DILLINGER: If you were going to hold Oktoberfest,

What would be your personal choice of months

In which to gahdamn sonofabitching hold it?

. . . Now, Baby Face, don't sulk. Don't pouty-pout.

BABY FACE: Your corkscrew conversation burns my ass.

You're always yinkin' on a string until

I swipe, and then "Ha-ha!"

DILLINGER: You take my point?

BABY FACE: You mean that thing you're jagging at me? Yeah,

I do. It's that I'm stupid once again.

Shuffle up them bicycles, Perfesser.

DILLINGER: Ante five.

BABY FACE: God*damn* it's hot. That's plenty,

Deal 'em, Johnny.

DILLINGER: Never call me Johnny.

BABY FACE: Yeh, you told me that already once

Or twice I think— You ever go to the zoo?

You know what a zoo is, don't you, Johnny D.?

DILLINGER: I know and I've been. Refer to me as John.

BABY FACE: John, did you ever go to the zoo, perhaps?

Did you ever go to the toilet at the zoo,

John? Did you ever go to the john, John?

OK OK OK. Cheez, what a grouch.

I gotta go at least a double sawbuck.

Gimme four.

DILLINGER:        The limit on the draw

Is three.

BABY FACE:     Then why do they call it five-card draw?

DILLINGER: . . . Three, and four.

BABY FACE:                    Christ! Them's the ones I had!

DILLINGER: I hate the zoo.

BABY FACE:              I fold. The zoo? How come?

DILLINGER: Because the animals are all in prison.

BABY FACE: That's right! I never thought of that! My deal.

The ante's twenty. All or nothing, Ma.

Can you imagine doing your time and people

Lug their snot-nose runts around to pepper

Peanuts and other such garbage at your cell?

Pointing at your private parts and laughing?

I mean, because you wouldn't have no pants?

Hey, I know the guy who's got the biggest

Wallywacker in Chicago. Bet.

DILLINGER: I guess you got down on your knees and

measured.

BABY FACE: Jimmy Lawrence.

DILLINGER:                    Twenty. Never met him.

BABY FACE: Yeah? Because I'm pretty sure he knows

Old Anna—fold—and Anna knows him back.

. . . She never mentioned Jimmy with a giant

Rutabaga hanging down right here?

. . . When you and her are cuddling do you feel

As like you're throwing toothpicks down a well?

Ah, me.

DILLINGER:    Dollar ante. Ante up.

BABY FACE: Perfesser, are you dealing out your ass?

'Cause shit is all I'm seeing here. Three. Four.

DILLINGER: Take six!

BABY FACE:            My deal.

DILLINGER:                    You call that shuffling?

BABY FACE: Ante up. Uh-uh. One hundred yoo-ess

Smackeroos, Perfesser. Go on, bet.

DILLINGER: Screw, chump. I won't ante half my wallet.

BABY FACE: John D. ain't no Rockefeller, huh?

Ante up, John. Ain't you got *one* ball?

. . .'Cause Anna Sage and Jimmy Lawrence made

An item and she used to walk like this.

WHAT'S OUT THERE!

DILLINGER:                        Nothing. Nothing's out there.

BABY FACE: I thought Wisconsin was cool beside the lake!

I'm sweaty-grimy in my creases!

DILLINGER: Maybe if you didn't hop around the place

Like ants was in your asshole.

BABY FACE:                        It ain't ants.

It's more invisible than ants. It's muggy

Fuggin' Fahrenheit. It crawls down *in*—

And *pisses*. That's what sweat is. Sweat is piss

That crawls out holes all over you.

DILLINGER:                        Amen.

BABY FACE: Workin' the Loozyanna voodoo on me.

Givin' me the hoodoo heebie-jeebies.

DILLINGER: You're a pistol. You're a sketch.

BABY FACE:                               My ass.

When your little Anna was hooked on Jimmy Lawrence

She sparkled in her eyes and walked around

Like she was bent from riding on a ox.

Ha ha ha ha ha! Shut up! Shut up.

—I mean it, John. Shut up. There's something out there.

Jeez! I got a headache up my ass tonight.

DILLINGER: We're supposed to be having fun, remember?

BABY FACE: I know—I got a bad condition, Doc.

Since when I was small and caught a dose

Of chicken rabies.

DILLINGER:                Chicken rabies, is it?

BABY FACE: That's the stuff. There ain't no remedy.

DILLINGER: Course not. All creation knows the dreaded

Chicken rabies gets you permanent.

BABY FACE: I got it at the carnival.

DILLINGER:                               Alas!

BABY FACE: There's nothing as worse as carnival chicken rabies.

WHO'S OUT THERE?

DILLINGER:                       Sit down! There's no one there!

BABY FACE: I SMELL YOU VOODOO BASTARDS.

DILLINGER:                                              Put that

down.

—Two-bit Tommy and his tommy gun.

BABY FACE: I GOT A WALAPALOOZA OF A HEADACHE.

DILLINGER: WHAT'S YOUR PROBLEM?

BABY FACE:                                    I don't know! The

doctor says

I'm cracked from my caboose to my cabeza.

DILLINGER: You don't need a gun. You need a girl.

BABY FACE: You gonna lend me Anna? She's too . . . roomy.

DILLINGER: Is she? Well, at least she didn't bolt.

BABY FACE: Aah, Helen hadda see her mudder.

DILLINGER: See her out of two black eyes.

BABY FACE: She yakked and I smacked her lightly. Seems
     to me
   She's one of those bleeders. It's inherited.
   Lucky for her a gentleman just employs
   The open hand. There ain't no stand-up women.
   I miss Suzette Petunia. My one true love.
   —Hilarious, I'm sure. Your deal.

DILLINGER:                     Your deal.

BABY FACE: I ain't letting go of my Sweet Suzette.
   I named this baby after her. Deal faster!

DILLINGER: Wasn't she thirteen?

BABY FACE:              I been a dirty old man
   Ever since I was a little boy.
   Shit! I want three cards.

DILLINGER:           O yaz O yaz.

BABY FACE: You gonna bet? You sure? You out of eggs
   Between your legs?

DILLINGER:           You're out of dollar bills.

BABY FACE: I'm sitting there, Suzette's in her brand-spang
    nightie,
   Got one leg up on the coffee table,
   I can see it all, her pretty package,
   I'm counting over a mess of gems from a little
   Deal I made with a jeweler over in Hammond,
   Swapped him a forty-four pellet in his ass,
   She's showing me her beauteous clam and saying,

"Everything you gaze upon is yours."
I say, "And this stuff too, my lovely prostidoot,
This which you gaze on, all these jewels are yours."
*She* don't know what a prostidoot means. —The cops
Break in! They got us by the hair, "OK,
Explain us who belongs to these bright baubles."
Suzette replies, "Them jewels is all mine, boys."
"They're stolen. Where'd you get 'em, sis?"
"Well, if they're stolen, I must've stole 'em, huh?"
—Yeah. She took the rap.

DILLINGER:                    You're proud of it.
BABY FACE: Judge in Hammond threw her five years flat.
    . . . She says, "It all belongs to you, sweet boy."
DILLINGER: Jesus Christ. I don't think you've got
    Not one stray speck of decency in your blood.
    —That's right, there's a blank pan for you.
    No idea what I'm talking about.
BABY FACE: Man O man, she fit me like a sock.
    I'll ride that filly like a dandy little jock!
    Oooooo she suck me like a Model O.
    A suction sweeper. Hoover. Model O.
    Mmmmm, my Hoover got the Quadraflex:
    "It agitates for double the brushing action!"
    "It beats as it sweeps as it cleans." I say!
DILLINGER: Hoover's gonna suck *you* up one day.
    Say, Rubert, can't you see the age has turned?
    These guys are coast to coast with all state lines
    Erased.
BABY FACE:   That Hoover hasn't got a gun!
    These G-bums ain't allowed to carry weapons.

"Hello, Nelson." "Howdy, Hoover"—BOOM!

It don't seem fair! But I don't make the rules.

DILLINGER: If he needs a gun, they'll vote him a Howitzer.

BABY FACE: Every time one thing goes wrong they pass

Some kind of law.

DILLINGER:               It's goddamn infantile.

BABY FACE: Exactly. What a buncha swaddling children.

DILLINGER: Give me men for my enemies!—not these

Schoolgoers and churchgoers and voters

Suckling on a giant perpetration.

BABY FACE: What what WHAT are we discussing, John?

DILLINGER: The lie, the fraud, the giant fairy tale.

Our entire history. For instance,

The possibility that John Wilkes Booth

Is innocent of any crime would merit

Scrutiny.

BABY FACE:      Well, you can scrutalize

The page from Sears and Roebuck I just wiped with.

DILLINGER: . . . It's not my deeds that poison me. It's all

The mucus of the slugs like you my deeds

Surround me with. I pass out drunk and wake

with you and Hoover wriggling over my lips.

BABY FACE: Mmmmm, lovah boy! Kiss my wriggle!

DILLINGER: We're revolutionaries.

BABY FACE:                    O yeah? Where's

The revolution? You can just point.

DILLINGER: We stand up for the man with empty pockets.

BABY FACE: I'd pick his pockets, if they wasn't empty.

That's my whole philosophy in a nutshell.

DILLINGER: The nutshell's on your shoulders.

BABY FACE: Mi mi mi,

    [*sings*] *O, the G-men had no guns in Kansas City,*

    *Mowed 'em down like wheat before the scythe,*

    *The G-men had no guns in Kansas City,*

    *And that's why there's three less of 'em alive.*

DILLINGER: That Pretty Boy Floyd, he fixed their stuff, all right.

BABY FACE: Floyd was not the guy in Kansas City.

    They're after him for what he never did.

    They'll end up catching him, too, and then he'll swing.

DILLINGER: Or fry.

BABY FACE: Or sizzle.

DILLINGER: Or stretch.

BABY FACE: His eyes will bug.

DILLINGER: He'll get as purple as a summer grape.

BABY FACE: He never shot those guys. Tough luck.

DILLINGER: Who did the deed?

BABY FACE: The world's so scared

    Nobody's talking, John, but I know for *dead*

    That one of 'em was Big-dick Jimmy Lawrence.

DILLINGER: Jimmy Lawrence?

BABY FACE: Anna's paramoor!

    He laid 'em down like wheat before the wind.

DILLINGER: So if the G-men spiced old James with lead

    That'd only be the simplest form of justice.

BABY FACE: Shut up! Guys like you and me should never

    Call for justice. What if the Devil hears?

DILLINGER: There ain't no Devil . . . What are you looking at?

BABY FACE: Look into my eyes. There's nothing here.

    There ain't no soul. Just two black dots. O yeah!

DILLINGER: Can that noise, Prince Albert. You're not Lucifer.

BABY FACE: I ain't Lucifer, I'm just the proof

       He walks the night and steals the souls

       And gnashes them down laughing—FREEZE! I SEE YOU!

DILLINGER: It's two a.m. What could be out that window?

BABY FACE: Nighthawks.

DILLINGER:             Nighthawks?

BABY FACE:                    Werewolfs.

DILLINGER:                        Werewolves?

BABY FACE: Look,

       It's voodoo doctors out to rob me of

       My guts and oysters for their ceremonies.

       We're too near the Mississippi River!

DILLINGER: What? Take yourself a slug and get a grip.

BABY FACE: That Creole sorcery!—with roots from under

       The gallows and dirt from witches' graves in tiny

       Tins tied up with string. And babies dragged out

       Dead from their mother's basket in a whorehouse.

DILLINGER: Dragged from their mother's basket?

BABY FACE:                       Not-yet babies,

       Floating in jars of rum!

       When I'm buried they'll come a thousand miles

       To steal my marker and my dirt. I'm bad.

       Jesus Christ pukes at the sight of me,

       And Satan hides in Hell when he sees my shadow.

       Every roll I throw, it comes up snake-eyes.

       Black cat crossed my path last night and snarled

       And died. My mama never even named me—

       Only spit in my face and laid a curse.

DILLINGER: Fetuses hunching in formaldehyde . . .

BABY FACE: Say, Perfesser. Foot-and-a-half-long words.
Remember what your aunt Matilda says—
"Never use words no longer than your whizzer."
In your case, shrink them down about this size.
Say, now: Jimmy Lawrence—

DILLINGER:                          I rob banks.
I rob banks, and if they ever catch me—
*Which* they'll never—they won't catch me alive,
I'll go down fighting.

BABY FACE:                    What a load a bull!

DILLINGER: I'll face my chasers and die my death with two
Bollocks full of red blood in my sack
And a couple pounds of government-issue lead
And copper peppering my meat.

BABY FACE:                          O Jeez,
Somebody hand me the gut wrench before I lose
My breakfast lunch and dinner.

DILLINGER:                          We are bandits.

BABY FACE: Finally something we agree about.

DILLINGER: Bad and good stand always eye to eye.
The law curses us and blesses them,
But we're all laboring in Satan's vineyard.
We take, but they guard bigger takers;
We march on our own orders, they obey
The orders of the big boss criminals;
We commit crimes and do our time like men,
They perpetrate injustices and breathe
Steam on their badges and rub up a shine. —What's that?

BABY FACE: What's what.

DILLINGER:                Shut up.

BABY FACE:                      I am.

DILLINGER:                   Shut *up*.

BABY FACE:                         I *am*.

DILLINGER: What's going on out there in west Wisconsin?

BABY FACE: It's just a coupla guys. Them two from Quincy.

DILLINGER: Yeah, but over there—no, *there*—you see

That shadow leaning against that car?—now that's

A gun wrapped up in his coat, or I ain't white.

BABY FACE: You're white as rice.

DILLINGER:                   That is a low-down lawman.

BABY FACE: That's a carload of 'em.

DILLINGER:                   That ain't the only car.

What are we gonna do?

BABY FACE:                Excuse me, there?

DILLINGER: What's our plan of escape?

BABY FACE:                      Excuse? Excape?

We're gonna shoot it out!

DILLINGER:                   O no we're not.

BABY FACE: Do you see this? Observe. Now see that cop?

. . . Now see the way that cop is sort of dead?

. . . Get off the floor!

DILLINGER:                Don't talk to me! Don't talk to me!

BABY FACE: Gee, Ma, it's rainin'!

DILLINGER:                   I don't want to die!

BABY FACE: O looky there, they shot the guy from Quincy!

DILLINGER: I *told* you next time they'd have Howitzers!

BABY FACE: I'm gonna shoot the other guy from Quincy!

. . . O jeez, they're shooting up my brand-new Stutz!

DILLINGER: Look. They're all around us. Let's surrender.

BABY FACE: . . . SEND FOR REINFORCEMENTS, G-MEN
    BASTARDS!
    YOU AIN'T PUTTING ME IN YOUR DIRTY ZOO!
    YOU THINK I'M A GIRAFFE? THEN WHAT'S THIS
    HERE?
    DOES THIS LOOK LIKE THE PROPERTY OF A
    GIRAFFE?
    GOD BLESS JOHN THOMAS!

DILLINGER:                         Who's John Thomas?

BABY FACE: Didn't he invent the tommy gun?

DILLINGER: General Thompson invented the tommy gun.
    . . . Nelson, Nelson, you're just aggravating
    Half the U.S. Army. Let's talk terms.

BABY FACE: What's yer poison, Johnny? Bullets, or bullshit?

DILLINGER: I'd rather be in prison than the grave.

BABY FACE: Either place, you rot. WE'RE WAITIN', G-MEN.

DILLINGER: Signal them.

BABY FACE:                No white flag, chump.

DILLINGER:                     Come on!

BABY FACE: Get up off that floor OR I WILL SHOOT YOU.
    Johnny, I am waltzing outa here
    With a sunshine smile and cunt-hair in my teeth.

DILLINGER: Even if we get downstairs, what then?

BABY FACE: You don't get it! THIS IS A SHORT RIDE.
    We're in the funhouse—here's the accelerator.
    . . . All right, Perfesser, point the thing and shoot.

DILLINGER: . . . Have you done this much?

BABY FACE:                   Not much.

DILLINGER:                     How much?

BABY FACE: Not very much at all.

DILLINGER:                              Me too. How many times?

BABY FACE: Actual face-to-face fighting with bastards with guns
    Like those?

DILLINGER:           I wasn't made for this.

BABY FACE:                                   I was!
    I live at the end of the world!
    They'll never take me alive!
    And the angels with a sword to bring it down
    Holy moly Molly on my head
    And the lion riding backwards on a smoking
    Dragon and the Whore from Babylon!
    [*Sings*] *Gimme that old-time religion,*
    *Gimme that old-time religion,*
    *Gimme that old-time religion,*
    *It's good enough for me!*

BOTH [*singing*]: *It was good for the Hebrew fathers,*
    *It was good for the Hebrew fathers,*
    *It was good for the Hebrew fathers,*
    *It's good enough for me!*

DILLINGER: Give 'em hell! I love a shooting gallery!
    And this is the real McCoy!

BABY FACE:                       Do you want real?
    DO YOU WANT REAL RIGHT UP YOUR ASSHOLE,
    MELVIN?

DILLINGER: TAKE THAT, PURVIS! This is glorious!

BABY FACE: Gunplay is funplay! Come on, Johnny.

DILLINGER: Where do you think you're going, idiot?

BABY FACE: You think I'm staying here and going to jail?

DILLINGER: We can't escape from here. But I escaped
    From jail last March. And I can do it again.

BABY FACE: They don't want us jailed, they want us dead,
   And that's what they'll get! And them dead too!
*He exits walking backwards while firing toward the window.*
BABY FACE [*singing*]: *It's gonna take us all to Heaven,*
   *It's gonna take us all to Heaven,*
   *It's gonna take us all to Heaven,*
   *It's good enough for me.*
DILLINGER *is alone with the bound young woman.*
DILLINGER: One more drum, Ma, then it's back to prison.
   [*Fires out the window. Then all is quiet. After a pause,*
   *he sings.*]
   *'Twas midnight and moonlight the hour I departed*
   *And left her to fend for her own*
   *My horses and all that I had on the earth*
   *I'd have wagered that I would return.*
G-MAN'S VOICE [*O.S., through megaphone*]: DILLINGER AND
   NELSON! (God, that's loud.)
   COME OUT. YOU'RE SURROUNDED. THERE IS NO
   ESCAPE.
DILLINGER [*singing*]: *Hands with a touch*
   *That could calm the little lambs*
   *Voice like a chime in the churchyard*
   *Eyes the same color*
   *As her straw-colored hair*
   *I'll never forget you I swear.*
G-MAN'S VOICE [*O.S., through megaphone*]:
   TWO MINUTES, THEN WE'RE COMING IN. GIVE
   UP!
   COME OUT BACKWARDS WITH YOUR HANDS IN
   THE AIR!

DILLINGER [*singing*]: *The shape of her shadow so soft in the*
*moonglow*
*Did waltz on the frost on the ground*
*The tears on her cheeks shone like diamonds*
*She mourned but she made not a sound.*
[*Meanwhile,* BABY FACE *reenters very stealthily by the*
*same way he exited, with his tommy gun and a white,*
*wet lily. In silence he waits for the song to end.*]
*Hands with a touch*
*That could calm the little lambs*
*Voice like a chime in the churchyard*
*Eyes the same color*
*As her straw-colored hair*
*I'll never forget you I swear.*

BABY FACE: Grandma taught me Father Who Art in Heaven,
And I felt it right down in, this feeling of being saved,
Like all the world was rescued, like as if
Angels with wings swooped down here and
Carried us away from these guns through the stars.
Grandma taught me to pray,
"Let me awaken as Jesus in every last part
Of my body." Whattaya think of that?

DILLINGER: . . . Do you realize for two and a half long days
You've done nothing but drink my booze and talk
About your pecker and his pecker and her pecker?

BABY FACE: Listen to what I'm telling you.
This is the news that I'm bringing.
There's nobody out be*hind* the place!
I went all the way to the lake and had a piss.

The coppers never even heard me tinkle.

Maybe there *is* a God to love us, John.

DILLINGER: Bull. Go out for real, and see what happens.

BABY FACE: I *went* out, John. I tiptoed out and took

A whizzer in the lake and shook it off

And tiptoed back to tell ya.

I brung you a lily, John.

DILLINGER:                          I am goddamned.

BABY FACE: Them G-men don't know how to surround a house!

G-MAN'S VOICE [*O.S., through megaphone*]: SIXTY SECONDS,

BOYS, AND THEN IT'S OVER!

COME OUT BACKWARDS WITH YOUR HANDS IN

THE AIR!

BABY FACE: They're spreading out! We gotta move, or else!

*They tiptoe out, leaving the young woman bound and alone in*
*the room.*

G-MAN'S VOICE [*O.S., through megaphone*]: THE HOUSE IS

COMPLETELY SURROUNDED. GIVE IT UP.

AS SURE AS YOU'RE BORN, WE'RE GONNA GET

YOU.

DON'T TRY TO THWART THE LAW. WE JUST

KEEP COMING.

AS SURE AS YOU'RE IN THAT ROOM, WE'RE

GONNA GET YOU.


BLACKOUT


- END -